100% Right 50% of the Time
Yossi Yassour

Producer & International Distributor
eBookPro Publishing
www.ebook-pro.com

100% Right 50% of the Time
Yossi Yassour

Translation from the Hebrew by Sarah Winkler

Contact: yassour@ruppin.ac.il
ISBN 9798712996919

100%
RIGHT
50%
OF THE TIME

HOW TO PREVENT FALLACIES
IN DECISION MAKING

YOSSI YASSOUR

CONTENTS

INTRODUCTION

Decision theory is a relatively new academic field. During the 40s and 50s of the 20th century, decision theory was considered a branch of game theory, a purely mathematical field assuming complete rationality and bearing hardly any applications in our emotionally filled day-to-day lives.

In 1968, a book written by Howard Raiffa titled *Decision Analysis* was published, and was essentially the first book to present decision theory as a field of its own. Raiffa's book was also completely rational. He used decision trees and utility functions and barely mentioned emotion or intuition as part of the decision-making process.

In 1975, when I was a young student at Harvard University in the United States, I met Professor Raiffa. He was my teacher at the time, and I told him that I was interested in studying decision theory—not only the mathematical and statistical aspects, but to integrate emotion as well. "By the way," said Professor Raiffa who knew I was Israeli, "there are two Israelis who are doing wonderful work in this field—Amos Tversky and Daniel Kahneman."

This was my first time hearing the names of these two Israeli psychologists, who four years later, would publish the article *Prospect Theory*, which drastically altered the face of economic theory and was cited more than any other article in the field.

Tversky and Kahneman were already well known as prominent

professors of psychology at The Hebrew University of Jerusalem. They published a few articles in the prestigious journal *Science* about consistent errors occurring in decision making. However, at that time, the connection had not yet been made between quantitative, rational, and statistical decision theory—which determines how one should make decisions, and is part of operations research, the mathematical subject I studied in business school at Tel Aviv University—and emotional, psychological, and intuitive decision theory—which reveals how people actually behave versus how they are supposed to behave.

Meanwhile in 1978, Herbert Simon was awarded the Nobel Prize in Economic Sciences. Simon, who was the first psychologist to win a Nobel Prize, posited that the rational assumptions that formed the basis of game and decision theory are unrealistic, and he went on to coin two terms that currently serve as cornerstones in decision theory: **bounded rationality** and the **satisficing principle**.

Simon claimed that even if we wanted to, we wouldn't be able to make completely rational decisions. Although we act rationally in principle, due to the lack of time and our inability to evaluate all the possible results, odds, and risks, our rationality is limited and incomplete, and therefore, is a **bounded rationality**.

Satisficing is the way in which we reach decisions. We don't end up marrying the smartest woman or the handsomest man that exists, because in order to do so, we would need to meet every single human of the opposite sex in the world! (And even if we do end up meeting all the possible candidates, we would probably reach age 90 by then, and the person that we choose may not even want to be with us…)

Therefore, based on the **satisficing principle**, we marry the first person who satisfies our minimum requirements. When a person meets someone who is smart, attractive, sensitive, and wealthy enough, they'll marry them.

The satisficing principle can also be illustrated through the following story:

A man wants to buy a computer. He can buy a one today with 100 GB of memory and a 20-inch screen for $1,000. If he waits a month, he will be able to buy a computer with 150 GB of memory and a 22-inch screen for $950. If he can resist and not buy it, after another month's time, he could buy a computer with 300 GB of memory and a 28-inch screen for $800. Wouldn't it be worth waiting a month or two in order to buy a much better computer at a much lower price? But those who don't purchase and wait for the next sale will never have a computer...

Those who want to buy a computer but constantly wait until a later date when a better and cheaper computer will become available, give up immediate pleasure in anticipation of greater pleasure in the future. But it could be that they will never reach that point of pleasure. The **satisficing principle** states that the moment we have the opportunity to buy a computer that is cheap and attractive enough—we buy it. There will always be a better computer, and a wealthier man, and a more attractive woman, and a newer car.

Another important principle in the field of decision making is **the reference point**: a point relative to which we feel good or bad, regret or disappointment, victory or loss, success or failure.

As a regular traveler, both by choice and on behalf of the Israeli government and other bodies, I often stay in developing countries. I especially enjoy traveling to the Far East and experiencing the full force of the vibrant Asian markets. Amidst the hustle and bustle, vibrant colors and the abundance of sights and tastes, I learn a lot about how purchasing decisions are made.

The intercultural encounter and the strong purchasing power of the dollar against local currencies do not dampen the sense of satisfaction I feel at the end of an endless bargaining exchange, even if the "huge deal" I got only involves saving a few pennies extracted from the clenched fist of an elderly peddler on the outskirts of Sri Lanka.

A few years ago, I went on vacation with my wife to the island of Ko Phi Phi in Thailand. We found a room at the Holiday Inn for $60 a night. The room was lovely. We sat on the porch at sunset and watched the sun slowly set over the waters of the Andaman Sea. We drank the cocktail served to us at the hotel in complete serenity. The fruit basket on the table in the room was full of exotic fruits. The feeling was wonderful. I told my wife how happy I am in our life together and how much I enjoy traveling with her.

We spent a quiet afternoon reading and hiking on the white beach adorned with palm trees, and in the evening, we went out to eat at a fish restaurant near the hotel. It was a warm and pleasant evening, and we sat down at a table overlooking the water. Suddenly another Israeli couple entered the restaurant.

"Are you Israelis?" They recognized us immediately. We were forced to admit that we were.

They continued and asked, "Could we sit with you?" They looked nice so we added two chairs to our table and ate together.

"Which hotel are you staying at?" they asked us.

"At the Holiday Inn."

"We are also. Which room?"

"301."

"We're in 401. Does your room also face the sea?"

"Yes."

"40 dollars is a great price for such a room, don't you think?"

At that very moment, the fantasy vacation came to a screeching halt. For the remainder of the meal, I was angry with my wife that we didn't manage to find a cheaper room. The many years of love were forgotten, the calm afternoon cocktail was forgotten, and the burning

$20 per-night loss filled me with great anger.

This is a classic example of the effect the reference point has on our emotional state. After all, the encounter with the Israeli couple did not change my absolute situation in any way. The room remained the same, the sea was just as blue as before, the sunset was still spectacular, the cocktail remained delicious, and my wife did not change either. The only thing that changed was my relative condition - and relatively, I felt like a sucker.

This insight made me realize that I could use the reference point to make people feel better or worse, and as a good student, I decided to use it at the first opportunity.

Two years later, I went on a group trip with my wife, my sister and her husband, and some friends to Namibia, Africa. We visited the famous, pristine dunes and the magical beaches. The night before our visit to Etosha National Park, we settled into our bed-and-breakfast at one of the agricultural farms in the area. The rooms were good and in the morning, I woke up feeling refreshed and longed to go out to the nature reserve to see all the wildlife. My sister came out of her room and asked us, "Could you also not fall asleep all night because of the hard mattress?"

Oh no! I thought to myself. Her wrinkled face made me realize that we were on the verge of a difficult day. "Did you also not have hot water?" I fired a new reference point back at her. Upon hearing my words, my sister's face began to soften. Her anger about the hard mattress was replaced by a sense of empathy for my unfortunate situation, and her mood miraculously improved.

To this day, I have not told her that not only did we have hot water in the shower, but we also had, unlike the rest of the group, a hot tub in our room. This little lie helped us all start the day in the Namibian steppe with a smile.

This book deals with the various practical aspects of decision making and the different ways to prevent decision-making failures. Apart from personal stories and insights gained, the book also includes results from recent studies by many researchers. The first section deals with **probabilistic failures.** What are the chances that my married life will be successful? What are the chances that my startup will succeed? We make many mistakes while estimating probabilities, which will be discussed in this section.

The second section focuses on **ambiguity and certainty.** It raises questions such as the nature of verbal assessments and how we translate them into numerical assessments, our preference for ambiguity under different circumstances, and the various subjective factors that influence our probability assessments.

The third section deals with **risk taking.** Many people mistakenly think that taking risks is the same as gambling. While every bet contains risk, not every risk is a gamble.

The fourth section examines the **rational assumptions of decision theory,** such as the sure-thing principle, according to which, if a person prefers A over B under a certain condition, and prefers A over B even when this condition is not met, then they will surely prefer A over B regardless of whether the condition is met.

The fifth section deals with the **perception of results.** Most of it is based on the many years of hard work of Danny Kahneman, who won the Nobel Prize in Economic Sciences in 2002, and the late Amos Tversky. The two published many articles, the most important of which deals with prospect theory. It is hard to believe how two relatively simple graphs are such an important key to understanding our behavior in decision making and in life in general. The first graph is called the value function, and it describes the relationship between actual, objective results, and the subjective feelings that these results create. For example, the value function explains why there is almost no difference between a 29-year prison sentence and one of 30 years, but there is a huge difference between being ordered to do community service and a one-year prison sentence. In both cases, the difference is one year in prison, but the feelings in relation to that one year are very different.

The second graph is the subjective probability curve which describes the relationship between the objective probability that a particular event will occur versus its subjective probability, as we feel it. For example, this curve explains why there is almost no difference between a 35% chance of something happening and a 36% chance of its happening, but the difference between 99% and 100% is very significant.

The sixth section deals with the effects of **emotion and intuition in decision making**. One of the interesting questions that arises here is whether a marriage born of love, as is customary in the Western world, is preferable over a marriage made by matchmaking. Is it better to heed the emotion called love over the wisdom, experiences, and insights of one's parents? When is it better to use emotion when making decisions, and when is it better to use your mind?

This is my fifth book about decision theory. The first discusses decision making in organizational settings; the second book deals with emotions in decision making and focuses on the decisions of murderers; the third book is a novel about decisions and crime; and the fourth (*Rationality and Affect in Decision Making and in Risk Taking*) is a professional textbook dedicated to the field of decision theory.

PART I

PROBABILISTIC
FAILURES

1

What Do Gamblers and Basketball Players Have in Common?

The first fallacy that I would like to discuss in this book—which, for the most part, deals with failures experienced at the point of decision making—is called the **gambler's fallacy**. I will open with a question: Which number sequence is more likely to emerge in a lotto: 1, 2, 3, 4, 5, 6 or 12, 31, 23, 14, 8, 42?

Most people who are asked this question, if they lack a background in statistics, will choose the second option, claiming that a random set of numbers has a higher chance of turning up, and they will ask, "Have you ever heard of a lottery where the winning numbers were 1, 2, 3, 4, 5, 6?" The obvious answer is no. "That exactly proves it," they will claim. The ultimate response to this question, and a shrewd one at that, is, "And what about you—have you ever heard of a lottery where the winning numbers were 12, 31, 23, 14, 8, 42?" The difference is that if 1, 2, 3, 4, 5, 6 were chosen in a lottery, it would be considered unusual and out of the ordinary, and if the second number sequence was chosen, no one would think anything was unusual.

The **gambler's fallacy** deals with the question: Is randomness more prevalent than order? Is a random sequence more probable than a consecutive sequence?

The casino is the source for the **gambler's fallacy** phenomenon. Gamblers who choose not to participate in the game for a long while can be found standing around the roulette table. They are tracking the roulette numbers and waiting until five consecutive numbers land on the same color. Almost half of the roulette numbers are red and a similar amount of numbers are black. One can bet on either "red" or "black," and the chances of them winning are close to 50% (roughly 47.4% in the United States and 48.6% in Europe). Those standing on the side wait until five consecutive numbers fall on red, for example, and then they bet a large sum on black.

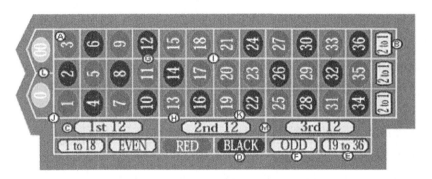

Typical roulette table in the United States

People who mistakenly behave according to the **gambler's fallacy**, assume that a dependency exists between independent events, as if Lady Luck bears a memory. The gambler's fallacy stands out in different aspects of life, for example the assertion that if rain hasn't fallen for three years, then a lot of rain will probably fall the following year. When students answer a multiple choice test, and they come across a slew of questions whose answers are all B, and if in the next question, they have to choose between B or D, they will most likely choose D. Traffic or small claims court judges tend to acquit those with a stream of previous convictions and convict those with a stream of previous acquittals.

Two more scenarios: One of two of your neighbors won the big lotto prize this week. What is more likely—that the winner is Andy from Apartment 4, who has been buying lottery tickets every week for the past ten years, or Ben from Apartment 6, who bought his first ever lottery ticket this past week?

Anna and Barbara are two 20-year-old women, and one of them has discovered that she is pregnant this month. What is more likely—that Anna, who has been engaging in unprotected sex for the past three years is pregnant, or that Barbara, who began having unprotected sex two months ago is pregnant?

Most people would say that it's more likely that Andy is the one who won the big lotto prize and that Anna is pregnant. These are two examples raised by Oppenheimer and Monin in their article "The Gambler's Fallacy in Retrospect."

The fact that Andy has been buying tickets for a decade and that Anne has been engaging in unprotected intercourse for three years bears no significance. It is the latest winning ticket that brought about a winner and the most recent sexual encounter that led to a pregnancy. The past is entirely irrelevant.

Is it more likely that a coin will land on *heads* the fifth time after landing on *tails* four times in a row? If your answer is yes, then answer the following question as well: How does a coin know that it has already fallen four times on tails? Where is its memory located?

On the other hand, a car that travels hundreds of kilometers without being filled with gas, will soon come to a stop. The one checking the gas tank can say with relative precision when the car will stop. Is there a similar way of checking when a coin will fall on tails? The answer is of course not. A coin doesn't have a memory, and therefore, the chances of it falling on tails after a certain sequence—assuming the coin isn't rigged with an asymmetrical weight balance or some other cheating mechanism—will always be 50%. The same goes for dice that land on a certain number at too high a frequency: one should check to see that there isn't a problem in the structure of the dice.

A woman gave birth to four boys, and is pregnant again. Are the chances of her having another son 50%, as they were before the first child was born? The answer here is a bit more complex. If the four-boy sequence is completely coincidental, just like the four times the coin landed on tails, then the chances of her having another boy are indeed 50%. That being said, there could also be a biological explanation here: For example, the father has trouble developing sperm with X chromosomes, in which case the chances of the woman giving birth to another son are higher. This case is similar to that of the rigged coin.

Moreover, regarding regular coins, people expect that what is meant to occur on average and in the long run, should occur immediately. Meaning, that if a coin landed on tails five times in a row, people expect it to fix itself and immediately land on heads! It's true that the coin should, on average and in the long run, land on tails in half of the cases, but it doesn't mean that the correction need occur immediately upon the sixth casting.

A 60-year-old man stood in front of a judge in traffic court. He was accused of driving through a red light at a junction. The man has 40 years of driving experience and hasn't once received a traffic violation. In his defense, the man claimed that the traffic light wasn't functioning properly, that the green light only stayed lit for two seconds before quickly switching to red with no yellow light in between, and as a result, he ended up entering the junction at a red light - the traffic light was at fault and not him. As a counter argument, the police officer who had cited the driver claimed that the traffic light was examined around a week after the incident and that it was found to be completely functional. Who should the judge believe? Should he punish the accused? It can be assumed that the police officer is not lying, and that the traffic light was working properly at the time that it was examined. At the same time, it could be that there was a temporary malfunction with the traffic light and that the driver is not lying either. Had the accused driver received previous traffic violations, it would be more reasonable to presume that he is lying. However, the fact that the veteran driver had zero prior traffic violations shows that he is generally a cautious driver, and therefore, the chances that he innocently ran through a red light are high.

If this is the case, then it can be said that people tend to believe that the probability of expected events to occur in the future are influenced by events that occurred in the past. And if the system has a memory, this is indeed so. For example, it is more likely that a repeat offender would commit the same traffic violation again than a cautious driver would commit one at all. In most cases, the system doesn't have a memory. The roulette wheel doesn't remember which number it spun in the last few rounds, and therefore, no previous results, not even the most immediate ones, have any influence on the chances of a specific number or color coming up in the next round.

Relying on past data is a very common method in estimating the odds, but failures are inevitable, like the **gambler's fallacy** mentioned earlier. One of the more famous fallacies is the **hot-hand fallacy** in basketball. This fallacy is harder to refute than the **gambler's fallacy**. Most people from the industry very much believe in the existence of the phenomenon called the **hot hand**, and they readily dismiss every statistician claiming otherwise, saying, "They don't know anything about basketball!"

The **hot-hand fallacy** refers to a phenomenon in basketball in which players, coaches, and most of all, fans are positive that at different stages in the game, a certain player will have a **hot hand**, and that the ball should be passed to them during this time so that they can shoot and make a basket. Often when players are asked what led to their success in a certain game, they will say that they had a hot hand and just made every shot, even from positions and situations where they don't usually score from. The player acts as if Gabriel the angel is soaring above the court, and with a touch of his invisible wing, blesses a player with good luck in the game.

If we momentarily ignore the angels, statistically speaking, the coach and the player think that someone who made four shots in a row has a higher chance of making the next shot than someone who made just two out of four shots taken in the last few minutes.

There are apparent logical explanations for this: "The player re-freshed his stance," "The player gained confidence," "The player's in good shape today," and the like.

Table 1, extracted from a famous study by Gilovich, Vallone, and Tversky, presents shooting percentages of players from the renowned Philadelphia 76ers team during their home games in 1981.

It is apparent from Table 1 that the shooting percentage after making three shots in a row is not higher than the shooting percentage after missing three shots in a row. In fact, for all of the players, the shooting percentage is lower, often even much lower, than the percentage after missing three shots, and on average, by less than 10%.

Player	Shooting percentages after making or missing shots in a row						
	After 3 hits	After 2 hits	After 1 hit	General	After 1 miss	After 2 misses	After 3 misses
Clint Richardson	48	50	49	50	56	47	50
Julius Erving	48	52	53	52	51	51	52
Lionel Hollins	32	46	46	46	46	49	50
Maurice Cheeks	59	53	55	56	60	60	77
Caldwell Jones	27	43	45	47	47	48	50
Andrew Toney	34	40	43	46	51	53	52
Bobby Jones	53	47	53	54	58	58	61
Steve Mix	36	48	51	52	52	56	70
Daryl Dawkins	51	58	57	62	71	73	88
Weighted average	46	50	51	52	54	53	56

Daryl Dawkins's shooting percentage rose dramatically after missing shots. This player joined the NBA directly out of high school; he was very young and lacked experience, which might have caused him to be extra sensitive about the shots that he missed. As a result, Dawkins would refrain from taking any shots after a series of misses unless he was absolutely sure that he would make them, directly contradicting the **hot-hand** theory.

One of the most common explanations for the **gambler's fallacy** and the **hot-hand fallacy** is that when people estimate probabilities, they tend to ignore all the available data and use only what is most accessible to them. Naturally, what is most accessible is recent data and not what appeared in the past.

An additional explanation is what is known as the **law of small numbers**. This is a humorous term coined by Tversky and Kahneman to paraphrase the **law of large numbers**—famous in the field of statistics—which states that a large enough sample will distribute similarly to the entire population. The **law of small numbers** expresses the psychological phenomenon where people come to faulty conclusions based on a small and unrepresentative sample, which can lead to generalizations, prejudices, and stereotypes.

The great Israeli psychologists, Amos Tversky and Daniel Kahneman, posed the following question:

A certain town is served by two hospitals. In the larger hospital about 45 babies are born each day, and in the smaller hospital, about 15 babies are born each day. As you know, about 50% of all babies are boys. However, the exact percentage varies from day to day. Sometimes it may be higher than 50%, sometimes lower. For a period of one year, each hospital recorded the days on which more than 60% of the babies born were boys. Which hospital do you think recorded more such days?

Only 21% of the people who were asked this question answered correctly. The rest erred and replied that more of such days were recorded in the large hospital or that both hospitals reported even numbers. The correct answer is that the small hospital recorded more days in which more than 60% of the births were male, and this is because the sample size is smaller, ergo the probability of deviating from the population average is higher. Every baby born in the small hospital makes up 7% of all the births that day, while in the large hospital, each baby born makes up 2% of all the births on that day. Therefore, each male baby born has a greater impact on the overall male birth percentage in the small hospital than it does in the large hospital.

Daniel Kahneman

Another example pertaining to sample size can be found in the field of athletics.

Every year, a team that is not considered one of the best wins the National Cup in soccer. These weaker teams never won in the National Soccer League. The reason for this is because National Cup games go by the method of "Single-elimination tournament", and the National League determines the winner according to the league's method, where every team plays each of the other teams three times. A weaker team's chance of winning against a stronger team is higher when they only play one game against each other versus when they play a series of games together. Therefore, it is not in vain that the leading team in basketball from one of the Mediterranean countries will prefer the final games to span a 7-game series, while the other teams request one game.

Read the following question:

> There are 60 red balls and 40 white balls in one sealed vase, and 60 white balls and 40 red balls in another sealed vase. A woman puts her hand into one of the vases and removes 3 balls, all of which are red (100%). Her partner reaches into the other vase and removes 10 balls, 7 of which are red (70%). Who among them should feel more certain that they put their hand into the vase where the majority of balls are red, the woman or her partner?

Tversky and Kahneman asked many people this question and most of them believed that there was a higher chance that the woman stuck her hand into the mostly red-balled vase. Here, too, people erred on account of the sample size. Removing 7 out of 10 red balls is a more impressive achievement than removing 3 out of 3. Consider a basketball player who makes 7 out of 10 shots taken versus another one who makes 3 out of 3. There is a higher chance that the one who made 3 out of 3 shots got lucky. As the number of shots increases, luck becomes less relevant, and the player's own skill gains increasing significance.

***

The Israeli researcher Ruma Falk tested the subject of randomness in an original way. She built two 12x12 grids, as can be seen in Figure 1. In both grids, 50% of the squares are black.

The researcher asked the subjects, "The sequence of one of these two grids was generated randomly, and that of the other was not. In your opinion, which grid had the randomly-generated sequence—the grid on the right or the grid on the left?"

Two grids presented for randomness judgement, black to white

If you are like most of the participants in the study, it's safe to assume that you would choose the grid on the right as the more random one. The grid on the left looks as if it contains sequences and has whole surfaces covered in the same color, and therefore, people tend to render it as not random.

In actuality, the left grid is the random one of the two. People mistakenly believe that if there is a 50% chance that a color will change, it is more likely to alternate in color than display a sequence of one color.

A very prominent mistake people tend to make is the conjecture that if two results are possible under conditions of uncertainty, the chances of each one being chosen is 50%. For example, when I ask farmers, "What are the chances that there will be a frost this year?" the popular response is, "Either there will be or there won't be." They believe that the odds are 50/50. But if a frost only happens once every 10 years on average in a specific area, the chances of one occurring next year are 10% and not 50%.

If you ask investors in the stock market, "What are the chances that a specific stock will go up?" they will answer "Either it will go up or it will go down; there are two options, therefore, the odds are 50/50." But the truth is that if the stock market is peaking, there is a greater chance that a specific stock will go up in value. And if the stock market is dropping, there is a greater chance that the stock will go down in value. It's not really 50/50.

On the same topic, there is a very well-known scenario regarding a game in which there are three doors. Behind one of the doors was a luxury car, and behind the other two were goats. In the game show, called *Let's Make a Deal*, once a contestant had chosen a door, the host (Monty Hall) didn't immediately reveal what was behind the chosen door, but opened a different door instead, behind which stood a goat. Since there were two doors with goats behind them, the host could always show the audience a goat. After the host exposed a goat behind one of the doors, he then gave the contestant the option of choosing again between the two remaining doors. The contestant could stick to his original choice or change his answer and choose the 3rd door.

Most people preferred to open the door they chose in the beginning. One of the reasons for this is because one who again chooses the door he chose in the beginning would be disappointed if he didn't win the car. But one who changes his original choice and goes for the 3rd door instead of the one he chose in the beginning, and then doesn't win the car, would not only be disappointed, but would regret not having stuck to his original fate - as he ended up choosing the door with the goat behind it when he could have chosen the door with the car.

An additional reason why people don't like to change their choice from the original door to the other one is because they are certain that there is an equal chance that the car will be behind either one of the closed doors. Such that if two doors remain, and the car is behind one of them, the chances that it will be behind the door that they chose is equal to that of the other door. In other words, 50/50.

However, surprisingly, this is incorrect! The chances that the car is behind the originally chosen door is actually 1/3 just like it was in the beginning of the game, and not 1/2. The game show host always opens a door with a goat behind it before opening the door that the contestant chose. The door that was not chosen, if intentionally opened to reveal a goat, does not provide any new information. And the chances that the car is behind the door that is still locked are 2/3 and not 1/2. The conclusion is that it is certainly worth switching over to the door that is still closed!

The picture on the following page was extracted from *The New York Times* which published a long exchange between Marilyn vos Savant, known for having the highest IQ in the world (228), and professors of mathematics who were arguing with her. Marilyn has a column in which she answers scientific questions posed by the readers. Her correct solution to the Monty Hall problem stirred a wave of cynical reactions from mathematicians and statisticians, who continued to earnestly claim that the chances are 50/50 after opening the first door.

The aim of presenting this game is to show that people very often mistakenly perceive there to be equal odds for two events, when in reality, the odds are not even.

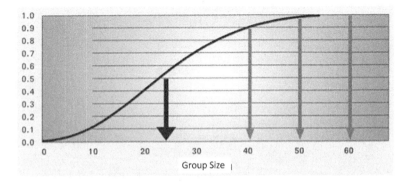

INTERACTIVE FEATURE
The Monty Hall Problem
Play Game   How It Works

You win! You get the fancy car (or at least a picture of one).

Try Again   See How it Works

And here's a famous riddle: There are 60 people in a room. What is the probability that at least two people have the same birthday? It seems that if there are 60 people in the room, and 365 days of the year, the chances are 60/365, or 1/6. However, this answer is incorrect. The correct answer is 99.4%—almost complete certainty. Figure 2 shows the probability of at least two people celebrating the same birthday for different group sizes.

Figure 2 – Probability of a shared birthday according to group size

One can see from Figure 2 that a group with 23 people already yields a 50% chance that two people share a birthday (day and month). In a group of 40 people, those odds reach 89%, and in groups of 50 and 70 people, the odds are 97% and 99.9%, respectively.

All of the examples above indicate that the manner in which we calculate or estimate probabilities is intuitive and not rational, and that in most cases, this method does not statistically yield accurate results.

To conclude this chapter, I will ask one of the more famous questions in the field, known as The Secretary Problem. There were 100 managers in a brand-new company. Each one was searching for a new secretary and each one wanted their secretary to be the best. A recruiting firm hired 100 people for the job, and now all that remains is to place them with a manager. Each candidate stood in a long line outside the company offices and waited to be placed.

The company's CEO chooses first. The CEO interviews the first candidate and can either hire them or decline their services and interview the next candidate. An interviewee not hired by the CEO continues on to be interviewed by one of the VPs, and the CEO can no longer hire this candidate. The CEO can interview as many candidates as desired until finding the ideal secretary. The question is, what is the best strategy the CEO can use to find the best secretary and what is the probability that the CEO will choose the best one out of 100 candidates?

Let's phrase the question a bit differently: You will write different numbers on 1,000 (or 10,000 or one million) pieces of paper ranging between negative infinity to positive infinity. Positive numbers, negative numbers, fractions, whole numbers—whatever you desire. Just tell me how many pieces of paper there are, and promise that there are no two identical numbers.

We will shuffle the pieces of paper really well, and I will need to guess which piece of paper contains the highest number. This is how I will do it: I will open the first piece of paper, look at it and declare that it does not contain the highest number. I will then open the second, the third, etc. At a certain point (before looking at all the numbers), I will stop and announce: "This is the highest number!" In your opinion, what are the odds that I will choose the highest number if you wrote numbers on 1,000 pieces of paper, and I have no idea what the range of numbers is?

There are those who innocently believe that if I randomly stop on one piece of paper out of 1,000, that the chances of me choosing the highest number are 1 in 1,000. This is the correct answer if I indeed choose the piece of paper at random, however, this is not what I will do. Here is the method that I will use, in the event that there are indeed 1,000 pieces of paper with different numbers.

After shuffling the notes really well, I will open 368 of them, one after another, and declare after opening each one that it does not contain the highest number.

As I open the 368 pieces of paper, I will remember which number was the highest of them all. Let's say that the highest number so far was 98 billion. I will then begin opening each of the other 632 pieces of paper. The first one that shows a number higher than the highest number from the first group (the first to be higher than 98 billion)—is the one I will declare to be the highest number out of all the 1,000 pieces of paper.

What is the probability that I will succeed? The answer is 36.8%. These high odds are true when dealing with 10, 1,000, or one million pieces of paper.

Try this method on 30 notes. Ask your children or significant other to write **any** 30 numbers on pieces of paper and mix them up really well. Open the first 11 notes (30 x 0.368 = 11). Recall which number was the highest. Continue on to open the remaining notes. Stop once you reach a number that is higher than the highest number from the first 11 pieces of paper. Now you will not be surprised to discover that in more than a third of the cases, you will succeed in guessing correctly.

Conclusions:

1. Those who believe in fate are likely to overlook accurate evaluation of the odds. Decisions that rely on fate ignore statistical probabilities for events. This disregard is akin to going against the odds and risks. Our deeds, and not fate alone, influence the results of our decisions.

1. Fate doesn't have a memory. There is no corrective or vengeful system on merely statistical events. We tend to interpret random results as if they compensate for deeds we did in the past. In reality, there is no connection between the events.

2. Contrary to independent processes in which there is no connection between one event and another, processes that do contain a memory system—meaning, those in which the situation can be measured at any point (such as the amount of alcohol in blood or gas in a tank)—their results do not depend on fate but on the state of the system and the direction that in which it is heading. A drunkard might get in a car accident not because of fate, but because of vodka, and a vehicle might come to a halt not due to bad luck, but because there is no gas left in the tank.

3. One should be careful not to regard fate as a trend. Oftentimes, a coincidental sequence can be assigned irrelevant meaning, such as discovering how many people in a certain city are ill with cancer and presuming that the area is riddled with radiation or polluted water. In reality, the phenomenon might be completely coincidental. Any conclusion derived from a small sample size is likely to be mistaken.

4. A large sample size is necessary in order to reach statistical conclusions. One who seeks to lose money in a casino should play multiple rounds of roulette betting with small amounts. One who seeks to win money, even though their odds are less than 50%, should play one round with a large sum of money. On the other hand, one who seeks to earn money in the stock exchange, should invest long term and not attempt to "strike it rich" within a few days. The reason is because the profit expectancy at a casino is negative, and one is more likely to win by playing one game, while the profit expectancy in the stock exchange is positive, and one is more likely to earn money by participating for a long stretch of time.

5. The chances of there being organized and disorganized sequences are equal. The probability that dice will land on 6 three times is equal to the probability that it will land on 3 and then on 6 and then on 4.

6. Usually two possible results don't share the same probability. Meaning, the odds are not 50%-50%. They can be 90%-10%, 60%-40%, or even 99%-1%.

2

Two Giant Men in Harlem and a Broken-Down Car

During Christmas vacation of 1975, I travelled with my wife to visit an aunt in a New York suburb next to Harlem. We drove from Boston, where I had been studying, in a car typical to Israeli students at the time—in other words, a big, old American car.

As we entered Harlem, the car sputtered with an odd groan, and came to a full stop. It was 6:00 at night and the city had just grown dark. An intense cold air began penetrating the car from outside, and the engine refused to start.

Suddenly, two giant men emerged. I said to my wife, "They're probably going to kill me and rape you." "Or the other way around," she answered frantically.

The two intimidating men approached the vehicle and asked in a pleasant tone, "Can we help you?" With our fragmented English, we tried to explain that our car broke down. They told us there was a garage not far from where we were and that it might still be open, and that if we wanted, they could help push our car there.

We were suspicious, but we didn't have any other option. We were stuck in the dark in a cold and strange city. Had someone found themselves in the streets of Harlem during Christmas break in 1975, they would have seen some small guy and two large men pushing an old American car down a dark road.

Luckily, the auto repair shop was still open. Our new friends and the shop owner grew fond of us and offered us a hot beverage. The car was repaired quickly, the price was extremely reasonable, and after thanking everyone from the bottom of our hearts and them wishing us a happy holiday, we continued on our way.

When we arrived very late to our concerned relatives, we told them what had happened, and they were shocked. "You shouldn't have driven through Harlem," they said. "What luck you had!"

It was in that moment when I first understood what prejudice really was and how it can develop toward a certain population, primarily minorities. Most of the criminals in Harlem are African-Americans. Black. But most African-Americans in Harlem are not criminals. Our experience was very cordial and friendly.

In the same way, one can say that most of the money lenders in Europe were Jews, but most of the Jews in Europe were not money lenders. Most lung cancer patients are smokers, but most smokers don't have lung cancer. Most drug addicts that use heroin and other hard drugs started by smoking marijuana and hashish, but most light drug users don't wind up becoming addicts...

A very common point of confusion among politicians and others is between the probability that X happens given that Y has occurred, and the probability that Y happens given that X has occurred. If a man has lung cancer, it is most likely the case that he used to smoke. But if a man smokes, the chances of him developing lung cancer are very small. This is the reason that some politicians fall victim to the **inverse fallacy** when they oppose legalization of light drugs claiming that their use will lead to the use of hard drugs.

A similar phenomenon is called the **prosecutor's fallacy**. If a murder suspect pleads guilty, it seems that the probability of him actually being the one who committed the crime increases. But what if real murderers don't cave under interrogation and don't plead guilty, while innocent people, who are not accustomed to interrogations and such pressure, actually confess to committing the crime? There is logic to the claim that the probability of an innocent man confessing to a crime that he didn't commit is higher than the probability of a guilty man confessing to a crime that he did commit.

A few years back, one of the employees at the college I teach at called to notify me that one of our students was suspected of being the serial rapist that was terrorizing the country. At that point in time, I had been volunteering at prisons for over twenty years. I got the details of this student and went to visit him at the detention center. I knew the warden and his deputy and they gave me permission to meet the suspect who had already spent three months in custody.

The student was astonished to see me. He told me that he had been beaten, starved, and humiliated, and that immense physical and emotional pressure was being put on him. One must recall that this was around the time when the public was in an extreme state of stress following multiple rape cases, that later turned out to have been committed by the infamous rapist Benny Sela. The matter also affected the police detectives who wanted to crack this difficult and horrible case and release the public from the threat of an evil rapist.

The student told me that in order to stop the pain, the fear, and the emotional and physical torture, he had almost confessed to a crime he hadn't committed.

We're familiar with other cases of murder suspects who confessed to a crime that later was revealed to have been committed by someone else. One of the most well-known Israeli cases is of Suleiman Al-Abeid, who was convicted in the Beersheba District Court for the murder of Hanit Kikos, a 17-year-old girl from Ofakim. He was also convicted by the Supreme Court when the case was revisited and presented in front of nine judges. It took 15 years after the murder for the Minister of Justice to recommend that Al-Abeid's sentence be shortened.

I must admit that when I first visited my student at the detention center, I did not know what to believe. Maybe he really was the terrible rapist? How would I know? When I met with him, he looked like a typical criminal. His face was unshaven, his eyes were sunken due to lack of sleep, and he looked miserable and desperate. I had then and I still have today complete faith in the police. But I knew then, like I know today, that every detective in the world is likely to err and get wrapped up in misinformed notions. And who could really know the truth?

After a while, the true rapist, Benny Sela, was caught, but the police weren't yet certain that he had been responsible for all of the unsolved rape cases, and they wouldn't agree to let the student go and return to his studies.

At the same time, the student's lawyer approached me and requested that the student be under my supervision while under house arrest at college. Not without hesitation, but knowing that the serial rapist had been caught, I agreed to the lawyer's request.

Eventually, it became clear that the student was not the serial rapist. He returned to his studies but was merely a shadow of his former self. With great effort, he completed his studies after dragging on for years, and I doubt very much that he will ever be able to undo the trauma he experienced when he was falsely accused.

Let's demonstrate the **prosecutor's fallacy** using a quantitative example in the following chart.

	Evil	Saint	Total
Confess	18%	3%	21%
Not Confess	72%	7%	79%
Total	90%	10%	100%

Table 2—Example of the prosecutor's fallacy

Let's assume that 90% of the accused are indeed guilty and 10% are innocent. (This data is according to the court rulings of the year 2000. During 2003 and 2004, the estimation of those guilty reached a whopping 99%).

Since the naïve and weak innocents confess to the crime more often than the stubborn guilty, the confession itself diminishes the probability of being guilty rather than raises it. Therefore, it's not for nothing that many jurists refuse to convict the accused based on a confession alone and demand further evidence.

The **inverse fallacy** is also the reason for **victim blaming**, according to which the victim is culpable for what happened to them, that they brought the crime on themselves. An example of this would be, "She should've known not to walk outside at night through dark streets. Why is she so surprised that she was raped?" It's true that most of the women who were raped at night had been walking through dark streets, but most women who walk at night through dark streets don't get raped.

Another phenomenon, **hindsight bias**, is connected to the ones mentioned above. People have the tendency to retroactively exaggerate what they would have estimated differently ahead of time. We will often hear or read of people saying things like, "I knew that would happen," or "The writing was on the wall." These are the words of the wise—after the fact, i.e., the words of soccer commentators. Most of the time the commentators are coaches who didn't really succeed and who currently earn money as specialists in critiquing other coaches and in analyzing games after they have ended. In the United States, this phenomenon is known as the "Monday morning quarterback." Events seem obvious in hindsight, even though it may have been very difficult to anticipate them in advance. **Hindsight bias** deters people from learning lessons because of the tendency to retroactively explain the phenomenon and the belief that they had understood it all along, when in reality, they only understood in hindsight.

Hindsight bias can be clearly observed in the stock market. Many experts exist today who claim that the global economic crisis and dramatic plunges in the global stock market could have been predicted. But where were these experts in 2008?

Similar to **hindsight bias** is another phenomenon called **creeping determinism**. This is when knowledge of the end result influences one's ability to recall consistent testimonies and evidence that explains the result. When we discover who the murderer was in a thriller movie, we suddenly remember all sorts of facts which—now—prove who the killer was all along.

In his book *The Naked Brain*, Richard Restak discusses how judgment is altered in hindsight. This is the process in which the brain "refreshes" its memory, not necessarily out of loyalty to truth. Restak references Gerald Zaltman's book *How Customers Think* in which he writes, "…moviegoers who initially expressed negative opinions about a film were later shown a favorable review and asked to describe their initial evaluation of the film, the one to which they had testified earlier... The moviegoers remembered initially judging the film in much more positive terms *after* they read the favorable review. Yet they remained completely unaware that they had distorted their memory of their original opinion. These consumers believed that they were repeating the exact same sentiments they had expressed the first time around. The reverse also occurred when consumers who initially expressed a positive opinion subsequently read a negative review of the film."

Consumers can be influenced to remember a past experience differently than how it occurred in a way that falls in line with a certain marketing message, and without them being aware that their memory had been altered.

In conclusion, we often claim that we predicted processes and events that happened in the past as if the writing was written on the wall, when really, we are actually being deceived by our memories. This results in a faulty reconstruction of the sequence of events as if it happened in reality.

There is an old Chinese idiom called *Lose the Axe, Suspect the Neighbor*:

> There was a man who lost his axe and he suspected the boy next door. He watched the boy walking—he had stolen his axe. His expression, his talk, his behavior, his manner, everything about him betrayed that he had stolen the axe.
>
> Soon afterwards the man was digging in his garden and he found the axe. On a different day, he saw the neighbor boy again. Nothing in his behavior and manner suggested that he would steal an axe.

Conclusions:

1. One should be wary of placing a label on a group of people merely because the members of said group share certain aspects that are also shared by most of the people in that group.

2. It's important not to pretend to understand events after they occurred. If we happened to be surprised, we should make an effort to understand what led to our surprise rather than try to claim that it wasn't a surprise at all and that we predicted the event from the beginning.

3. It's best to learn from mistakes that we've made in our past and not to blur them. It's befitting that a policeman who understood in hindsight that he was mistaken in his initial assessment, should try to find the source of his mistake rather than search for reasons that justify the error.

4. People can be influenced by events and information, and their memory has the tendency to change. They may think that the memory is authentic, when really it shifted as a result of information that was revealed only later. Someone who has a memory altered and was then hooked up to a lie detector, would be found to be telling the truth because the fact that their memory changed is unknown to them.

3

The Injured Soldiers from Lebanon and Simpson's Paradox

Which hospital is better—the Galilee Medical Center (GMC) in Naha-riya or the Rambam Hospital in Haifa? If we check the rate of recovery of injured soldiers that were brought to the two hospitals, we will find that GMC has a higher recovery rate than Rambam Hospital. But if we check the rate of recovery of lightly injured soldiers, we will dis-cover that Rambam Hospital has a higher success rate, and the same would be found with the severely wounded. The reason for this lies in **Simpson's paradox**—a statistical paradox stating that an inversion of a trend takes place when subgroups are combined into one group. The reason why the overall recovery rates at GMC are higher than those at Rambam Hospital is that most of the seriously injured arrive at Rambam, while most of the lightly injured arrive at other hospitals, rendering their recovery rate higher.

Let's take a look at another example: Table 3 deals with discrimina-tion between Black and White murderers and murders that occurred in the late 1970s in Florida.

We're talking about 637 murders, with one murderer and one murdered in each case. In total, there were 335 Black murderers who murdered

269 Black people and 6 White people, and 302 White murderers who murdered 17 Black people and 285 White people. Some of the killers were sentenced to death: 5% of the Black murderers and 7% of the White murderers.

	Black Murderer			White Murderer			Total		
Murdered	Black	White	Total	Black	White	Total	Black	White	Total
Total	269	66	335	17	285	302	286	351	637
Death Penalty	6	11	17	0	22	22	6	33	39
Death Penalty (%)	2%	17%	5%	0%	8%	7%	2%	9%	6%

Table 3—Data on the execution of Black and White murderers

White people in Florida cried out and demanded an investigation into the injustice done to them by law enforcement. The results of the investigation not only refuted the White people's claims, but proved that a double discrimination exists against Blacks: When a Black person is murdered, court houses treat the case more leniently than when a White person is murdered; and when a Black person is the murderer, court houses treat the case with greater severity than when a White person is the murderer.

When a White person is murdered by someone White or Black, death penalty rates are 8% and 17%, respectively. However, when a Black person is murdered by someone White or Black, the rates are 0% and 2%, respectively. Meaning that the murder of a White person is considered much worse than the murder of a Black person, with no significance to the color of the murderer's skin.

When a Black person murders someone White or Black, the death penalty rates are 17% and 2%, respectively. However, when a White person murders someone White or Black, the rates are 8% and 0%, respectively. Meaning that discrimination exists against Black murderers.

And here is **Simpson's paradox**: If Black killers are sentenced to death more often than White killers over a White person's death (17% versus 8%) and also over a Black person's death (2% versus 0%), how is it that overall, more White people are sentenced to death?

The explanation is similar to that of the hospitals: Since the White murderers kill mostly White people (285/302) and punishment for killing a White person is more severe, White murderers are sentenced to death more than Blacks overall, even though there exists clear discrimination against Black people.

Another example, easier to digest, is the apparent discrimination in accepting students to a higher education institution. Please see Table 4.

	Psychology		Business		Total	
	Boys	Girls	Boys	Girls	Boys	Girls
Applied	100	900	900	100	1000	1000
Accepted	6	108	360	80	366	188
Acceptance %	6%	12%	40%	80%	36.6%	18.8%

Table 4— University acceptance rates based on gender

Is there discrimination here in accepting girls? Or perhaps in accepting boys? And what do you think about the different departments—psychology and business? Do they show discrimination towards one of the genders?

The table analyzes 1,000 boys and 1,000 girls who applied to a university. Among the boys, 366 were accepted, but only 188 of the girls were accepted. There seems to be discrimination here against girls, but upon observing the two departments, one can see that the girls were actually treated favorably: Their estimated acceptance rate is double than that of the boys (12% versus 6% in psychology and 80% versus 40% in business).

The reason for the lower total acceptance rate for girls is because most of the girls (90%) signed up for psychology while most of the boys signed up for business, a department with a much higher acceptance rate (44%).

And a final example of **Simpson's paradox**: Table 5 shows data from two airlines in June of 1991, from 5 different airports in the United States, about flights that departed on time and flights that experienced a delay.

The data shows 3,274 flights from Alaska Airlines that took off on time and 501 flights that were delayed in departure. Ergo, 13.3% of the flights were delayed compared with America West Airlines who only had 10.9% of their flights delayed.

It seems as though America West Airlines is better, but if we compare the two companies at every airport, we will discover that Alaska Airlines is better than America West at each one of them. For instance, the percentage of delayed flights for Alaska Airlines at Los Angeles International Airport is 11.1% compared with America West's 14.4% of delayed flights at the same airport. At the San Francisco International Airport, the percentage of delayed flights for Alaska Airlines was 16.9% while America West Airlines experienced 28.7% flight delays.

	Alaska Airlines			America West Airlines		
	On time	Delayed	Delay %	On time	Delayed	Delay %
LA	497	62	11.1%	694	117	14.4%
Phoenix	221	12	5.4%	4840	415	7.9%
San Diego	212	20	8.6%	383	65	14.5%
San Fran.	503	102	16.9%	320	129	28.7%
Seattle	1841	305	14.2%	201	61	23.3%
Total						

Moore (2003), *The Basic Practice of Statistics*

Table 5 — Flight data of two airlines from five airports in
the United States

So if Alaska Airlines functions better than America West Airlines at each of the airports, how come their overall figures are worse?

The explanation is simple: Most of the America West flights depart from airports with pleasant weather, while most of the Alaska flights depart from airports with inclement weather.

In conclusion, when we make decisions based on a total sum of statistical data, such as total success rates of surgeries, standardized tests, court cases, or university acceptance rates, we are likely to assess them incorrectly. The proper way to examine such data is to consider each relevant subgroup individually and separately. For example, when discussing doctor and lawyer expertise, one should compare hard cases from easy cases; and when discussing university acceptance rates, one should examine each faculty by itself instead of analyzing all the data at once.

Conclusions:

1. One should refrain from comparing two large populations containing diverse sub-populations.

2. Comparisons among schools, hospitals, airlines, or populations in general should be made at the level of subgroups of the population instead of analyzing the population as a whole: First, we must determine whether our relative is seriously or lightly injured, then we will compare hospitals based on how they perform with the appropriate subgroup, and only then will we decide which hospital to take them to. This is because an overall comparison does not reflect the relative parts of each subgroup in the whole, and therefore, the overall picture obtained can often distort reality.

3. Sometimes, based on overall information, we perceive there to be discrimination against a certain population when, in reality, that same population may actually be favored. The acceptance rate of Arabic students to Israeli universities may be lower than that of Jewish students. Does this imply discrimination? It could be, but it could also be the case that most Arabic students apply for studies that are hard to get into like medicine, law, and accounting, while most of the Jewish students apply for studies that are easy to get into like literature and sociology. Admission rates should be compared at the level of the sought profession. And it may then turn out that admission rates of Arabic students in certain professions is higher than that of Jewish students, despite the initial information received.

4

Watching the Movie Jaws is More Dangerous than Swimming in Floridian Waters

Which is more dangerous—swimming at the beach in Florida or sitting at home and watching TV? On July 6, 2001, a shark attacked a boy on a Floridian coast. Two months later, on September 3, 2001, a shark attacked a couple in North Carolina. The man was killed and the woman was severely injured. An alert subsequently went out to all public beaches on the United States' East Coast.

Between the years of 1990–1997, 28 children died in the United States from fallen TVs. This number is four times greater than that of people who died from shark attacks over the course of the 20th century. The conclusion: It is more dangerous for kids to watch the movie *Jaws* on TV than to swim at beaches in Florida. (This example is a bit unfair since many more kids watch TV also for much longer periods of time than those who visit the beach, but don't let this fact ruin the example...)

When a shark attacks and kills someone, the evening news makes a big deal about it. The headlines are smaller when someone dies at home or in a car accident.

Some events are considered dangerous, like a beach day on a Florida coast or a flight, but these events are actually not dangerous at all, or at least much less dangerous than riding in a car on a Florida highway or resting under a coconut tree in Fiji.

In 2001, a number of envelopes were mailed within the United States containing spores of lethal anthrax bacteria. Five people died from exposure to the brown powder and 17 were left injured. Some of the envelopes were sent to members of the Senate, like the one depicted below, and the American public panicked. One must remember that this occurred very soon after the al-Qaeda attack on the twin towers in New York, and American citizens rushed in large numbers to get the Anthrax vaccine.

At the same exact time, a flu epidemic broke out in the United States. The Ministry of Health implored its citizens, mostly the elderly among them, to get vaccinated. Compared with the response to anthrax, the number of people who got vaccinated was very low. That same year, 2001, nearly 40,000 people died from the flu, 8,000 times more than the mortality rate for anthrax. The budget for the development of a flu vaccine for the following year was set at 283 million dollars, while the budget for the development of an anthrax vaccine stood at 5 billion dollars—18 times more than for the flu vaccine.

Why did the Americans make this mistake and rush to develop a vaccine for anthrax but not for the flu? And more pertinently, why did the American government invest so much money in search of a vaccine for anthrax, from which one person on average dies a year in the United States, and not for the flu, which is responsible for tens of thousands of deaths?

The reason is the impressions that these illnesses create and the circumstances in which infection occurs. A terrorist attack in the form of poisonous envelopes naturally grabs media attention more than an already well-known disease which primarily affects the elderly. A plane crash makes a larger fuss in the media than a car crash. The chances of dying in the United States from a car crash over the course of one person's lifetime is around 1 in 100. The chances of dying in the United States from a plane crash over the course of one's lifetime is 1 in 20,000. In other words, there is a 200 times greater chance to die in the United States in a car crash than in a plane crash. It has even been found that there is more of a chance of losing one's life in a car accident on the way to the airport than on the flight itself...

This phenomenon is called **availability bias**: An event seems more likely to occur the easier it is to recall or the more available it is in one's memory.

Let's try to understand this further by completing the following task. Take five seconds to think about all the country names you can think of that begin with the letter 'I.' Then do the same for the letter 'C.' List the country names you can come up with in Table 6 below. Try to limit yourselves to five seconds per letter. When five seconds are up, since you probably weren't able to think of all the options, write down your opinion of how many countries in total begin with that letter, including the ones you did and did not think about, and write the total number under line X at the bottom of the table.

Country names beginning with the letter			
C		I	

Table 6—Country names that begin with certain letters

Now, after you have written down names of all the countries you can think of, go to page 259 to see the correct answers—names of all the countries that begin with the letters 'I' and 'C.'

Are you surprised by the results? Many people err in their estimation of the number of countries because it is easier for them to remember countries that begin with certain letters and not with others.

Similarly, the study participants were asked, "What does the English language contain more of—words that begin with the letter 'R' or words in which the third letter is 'R'?"

Most of the subjects responded that there are more words that begin with 'R,' and the reason for this is because it is easier to think about such words and to bring them to memory. However, there are actually more words where the third letter is 'R.'

Generally, the way in which people assess the odds is largely based on their memory and ability to imagine similar events. This process relies on recalling events from one's memory, and the easier something is to recall or the more an event is engraved in the memory, the more likely it is that something which shouldn't necessarily be remembered will be remembered, which could potentially lead to misjudgment when evaluating the odds.

Conclusions:

1. The chance of being killed by a missile in Sderot (in Southern Israel) is less likely than that of dying in a car accident. Despite this, due to the news headlines of the events, people are much more wary of driving to the South during missile crises than of the actual drive itself.

2. When afraid of something, like a flight, bungee jumping, childbirth, or a missile, one should think about how many of these events occurred in the past and how many of them ended badly. Statistics in such cases can often serve as anxiety medication.

3. One must remember that some things are easy to recall or think about, but this does not mean that they are more likely to occur.

4. We rely on information that is most available—information that was most recently acquired or received in a manner that attracts attention or etched easily into our minds—and not necessarily information that is most important.

5

Some Rationality for the Ratio Bias

A Japanese professor named Yamagishi taught two classes at the Tokyo Institute of Technology. He asked his morning class, "What is the rate of people who die in Japan from cancer, heart disease, murder, and traffic accidents?" And these were the answers given by the morning class students:

Cancer: 24%
Heart disease: 24%
Murder: 14%
Traffic accidents: 18%

The night class was asked a similar question, but instead of requesting the rate in percentages, they were asked how many of these deaths occurred from a total of 10,000 deaths. The following shows the results from the night class:

Cancer: 1,286 (13%)
Heart disease: 1,512 (15%)
Murder: 487 (5%)
Traffic accidents: 893 (9%)

The night class's estimations were about half of those from the morning class. Is there a difference between estimations made in percentages than those made by other means?

Studies show that when we make a decision based on probabilities, we tend to focus on the numerator and neglect the denominator. This is how, for instance, it comes to be that most people (61%) prefer to participate in lotteries in which a prize is won if they get a white ball from a jar that contains 100 balls, 9 of which are white, over a lottery in which a prize is won when a white ball comes out of a jar that has 10 balls where only 1 of them is white. Odds of 9/100 are perceived as higher than odds of 1/10.

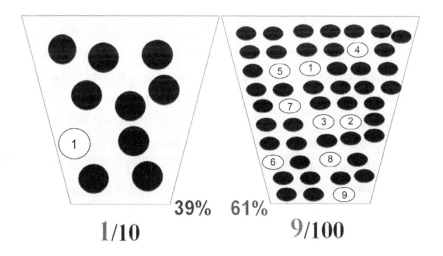

This phenomenon, titled **ratio bias**, is also found among the highly educated and experienced in their field.

Psychiatrists were asked if they should release a certain mentally ill patient from the hospital. Around 40% of the psychiatrists were opposed to the release when the individual's risk assessment of aggressive behavior was 20 out of 100 similar patients, meaning that out of 100 patients suffering from similar mental illness, around 20 of them were likely to act aggressively. But only 20% of the psychiatrists were opposed to the release when the patient's risk assessment for aggressive behavior was 2 out of 10, or in other words, when 2 out of 10 patients with similar mental illness were likely to act out aggressively. It turns out that the ratio 20/100 looks higher than 2/10. 20 out of a hundred dangerous mentally ill patients wandering the streets looks like a lot. Two out of ten doesn't seem so dangerous. The chances that I will meet one of them in the street look small.

When doctors were asked to evaluate a medical treatment involving a mortality rate of 176 people out of 1,000 patients, they perceived the treatment as having a similar rate to a treatment where 37 people would die out of 100. Meaning, 17.6% equals 37%.

Similar research was conducted with a jury. They were told that a murder took place in a certain store, and that the blood found in the store matches DNA to that of a suspect that shopped there frequently. A third of the jurists were told that the chances that the blood test was unreliable is 0.1%, another group of them was told that the chances were 1/1,000, while the third group were told that they were 2/2,000. Table 7 shows the different jury groups' estimation of the odds that the suspect was the source of the blood that was found at the crime scene.

Probability of a false blood test	Jury estimations that suspect matches blood source
0.1%	63%
1/1,000	43%
2/2,000	24%

Even though the three different statistical figures above are mathematically identical, they influence the jurists in very different ways. 0.1% seems like negligible odds. The chances that the suspect doesn't match the blood at the crime scene are insignificant. When we hear that there are odds of one in a thousand (1/1,000), we imagine one person—who is probably the suspect. But when we are told that the odds are two out of two thousand (2/2,000), there are already two individuals for whom the test could have been wrong. So maybe the second one is the murderer?

In all of the examples provided above, one can see how our attention is more focused on the numerator than on the denominator. Statistical data presented in different mathematical forms, such as 1%, 1/100, 2/200, 10/1,000, or 100/10,000, forges different sensations in our brains regarding the event's probability, even though all of the values are actually mathematically identical.

Conclusions:

1. When we hear estimations of probabilities provided in different mathematical formulas, we regard them differently.

2. When odds are presented in the form of a simple fraction, with a numerator and a denominator, the numerator grabs our attention more. Therefore, in order to arrive at an educated decision, one should play with the number, move it around into different mathematical forms, and see if our initial feeling about the risk assessment or probability changes. For example, if someone tells us that the odds of recovering from a disease without surgery is 1 in 10, before reaching a decision about the surgery, we should also think about it as 100 out of 1,000 people who recover. If we feel the same way about the surgery, we should stick to our original decision. However, if the change in how we frame it raises different feelings, we should think twice about the surgery.

6

Raise Anchor and Set Sail

Dan Ariely is an Israeli professor at Duke University in North Carolina. He served as president of the Society for Judgment and Decision Making from 2008–2009. His research is original and oftentimes humorous. His excellent book *Predictably Irrational* describes a series of original research studies which he and his colleagues conducted in the field of decision theory.

One day, Ariely came into class with a bottle of French wine, from the Côtes du Rhône harvest of 1998, and asks his students if they would be willing to purchase the bottle of wine for a sum higher than the last two digits of their social security number. After they answered, positively or negatively, they were asked to give a maximum price they would be willing to buy the bottle of wine for.

Students whose social security ID ended in numbers between 00–20 were willing to pay an average of 8.64 dollars for the bottle, and those whose ID ended in numbers between 80–99 were willing to pay an average of 27.91 dollars.

What is the reason that some of the students were willing to pay three times that of the other students?

The students did not know what the exact price of the French bottle of wine was. They had a rough estimation. Very rough. Let's take, for example, a student whose ID number ends in 05. This student was asked if they would be willing to pay more than 5 dollars for the bottle. After a short hesitation, they responded, "Yes. I am willing to pay more." "How much are you willing to pay?" Ask the student and they will answer, "Um … up to 7 dollars."

Now take, for example, a student whose ID number ends in 95. After asking whether they would be willing to pay more than 95 dollars for the bottle, they will say without hesitation: "No. I am willing to pay much less." "How much are you willing to pay?" Ask the student and they will answer, "Um … 30 dollars, maximum."

Dan Ariely

The last digits of the social security number served as an **anchor** - an unconscious anchored measurement. When people are asked to estimate a value of a certain factor, they set a specific anchor value and make decisions relative to it. For example, if we are asked how many people will die from traffic accidents in 2022, it can be assumed that the anchor we will use is how many deaths there were in 2021. We will then match estimations to this number, such as a rise in the number of cars on the road and construction improving the streets, and then we will reach a final assessment. However, a change in the anchor value will affect and alter our estimation.

When did Einstein first visit the United States? Before or after 1215? Before or after 1992? If Einstein was born in Germany in the year 1879 and died in the United States in 1955, it can be assumed that his first visit to the United States took place after he was born and before he died.

Despite this, those who were asked if his first visit to the United States was before or after 1215 estimated that his first visit was in 1922, and those who were asked if his first visit was before or after 1992 estimated on average that his first visit was in 1928. By the way, the correct answer is that Einstein's first visit to the United States took place in 1921.

Albert Einstein

We have many anchors in our world, both visible and hidden, that affect our decisions at every step of the way. Here is an example: In a certain experiment, Campbell Soup was being sold for 79 cents a box, when usually it was sold for 89 cents. The experiment was conducted in three stores with a sign next to the stand saying, "Campbell soup on sale—79 cents per can." One of the following sentences was also written on the sign: "No limit on purchase;" "Purchase is limited to 4 units per person;" "Purchase is limited to 12 units per person."

In the first store, which had no limit of the purchase quantity, each person bought 3.3 cans of soup on average, and in total, 73 cans were sold. In the second store, which had a purchase limit of 4 cans, each person bought 3.5 cans of soup on average, and 106 were sold in total. In the third store, which had a purchase limit of 12 cans, each person bought 7 cans on average, and the total number of cans sold was 188.

One can easily see that when the purchase limit is 12 cans per person, the average number of cans sold per person rose by 121%, and the total number of purchases rose by 157% relative to when there was no purchase limit. The difference lies in the concealed anchor value of the maximum number of cans allowed to be purchased.

An **anchor** doesn't have to be a number. It can be a package or the size of a vessel. People tend to buy beer in cases of six because that is how they are packaged, but they are able to be bought in smaller quantities. The amount of toothpaste we use is influenced by the length of the bristle cluster of the toothbrush. The size of the shopping cart at a supermarket also serves as an anchor. Some tend to buy what is on the shopping list and no more, while others go to the supermarket without a shopping list, wander through the aisles taking what looks good and then make their way over to the register with a full cart. Supermarket chains make their shopping carts larger for a reason. (It's just a shame that they don't fix the front wheel of the cart, that one that never moves as it should and leads the customer to push the cart diagonally, and thus shorten the time spent in the store…)

In conclusion, I want to show how the **anchoring effect** affects not only laypeople, but also professionals, and not only in experiments involving students, but also in the real market. The following example describes an experiment that was conducted with actual real estate agents.

The real estate agents received a file full of details about a specific house. The file included all the details of the house: quality of construction, occurrences of renovation, building materials used, names of the contractors, prices of other houses in the area, etc. The only difference among the agents was that some of them were told that the homeowners were asking to sell the house for $120,000, and some were told that the asking price was $150,000. These experienced real estate agents saw and assessed the house, read the heavily-detailed file, and were asked to sell the house. In the end, the average asking price for the first group, with the low anchor value, was $111,000, while the average asking price for the group with the high anchor value was $127,000, meaning, 14% higher than the former. All the remaining information about the house was identical and all the real estate agents were experienced and working in the field a long time.

And in a different matter: 16 judges with an average experience of 15 years as acting judges were provided a detailed description of a rape case. Half of the judges were told that a computer science student in his freshman year, who took upon himself the role of prosecutor, claimed that the rapist deserved a 34-month sentence. The rest of the judges were told that a student who lacked legal experience claimed that the rapist deserves a 12-month sentence.

The average punishment given by the real judges from the first group was 36 months of jail time, and the average punishment given by the second group of real judges was 28 months of incarceration alone. Even educated and experienced judges fell for the anchor trap. In conclusion, evaluating the size of numerical data depends heavily on the framework in which it is being evaluated. Without noticing, we are exposed to many anchors which lead us to evaluate data relative to that anchor: the number of items purchased at a supermarket is dependent on the size of the cart, the amount of toothpaste we use is dependent on the surface area of the bristles, and the price we agree to pay for a certain product is dependent, among other things, upon a different number that we are thinking about during the shopping experience.

Conclusions:

1. We use known anchor values when evaluating unknown data, and we usually fail to repair and adjust our assessments to include other factors.

2. While evaluating certain quantifiable variables, our consideration factors should not be swayed by anchors, whether they were set by ourselves or by others, known or subconscious.

3. One should consult with a number of people, preferably experts in the field, before conducting an evaluation. Even then, one should ask some of them a question without applying an anchor, ask others with a low anchor, and the rest with a high anchor, and only then arrive at a final assessment. The same is true for business deals such as selling an apartment or a car.

4. Many use anchors in marketing as a means of raising sales. These anchors serve, on the one hand, to raise the number of buying customers, and on the other, to make the product seem more enticing to buy. The farther away the price is from the anchor value that is depicted as the regular price, the more enticing it is to buy the product.

5. Anchors play a primary role in negotiations. In many cases, people are wary of providing an offer lest their offer be used as an anchor. They suspect that the sum they offer is higher than the initial sum the other party intends on asking for. And therefore, the initial price brought to the negotiating table will greatly impact the final result.

7

Who is Ruth?

One of the workers at a school was chosen at random from a list of employees. Ruth was chosen, a woman in her forties whose friends say she was really shy and introverted, very helpful in times of need, but showed little interest in people and in current events. She had a tendency for organization and cleanliness, and she focused a lot of her attention on small details.

From among those listed below, which do you think was Ruth's profession? Nurse, teacher, secretary, librarian, or psychologist?

In an original study conducted by Tversky and Kahneman and the dozens of times I asked my students and lecture participants, the vast majority believe that Ruth was a librarian. Apparently, many librarians fit the description above, and that is the reason why most people believed that Ruth was a librarian.

The **representativeness heuristic** is a phenomenon in which probabilities are evaluated based on a measure of imagination between the description of the particular case and a familiar image often shared among a particular population.

But in our case, the chances that Ruth is indeed a librarian are quite low. Why? Because the rate of librarians at the school is low. Even if 100% of librarians are indeed shy, there are apparently more shy teachers than there are shy librarians. To keep matters simple, let's assume that 100 people work at the school, and they are either teachers or librarians. 98 of them are teachers and the rest are librarians. Even if only 5% of the teachers are shy (5) and 100% of the librarians are shy (2), of the seven shy people, five are teachers and two are librarians. Ergo, the chances that a shy person is a teacher are 5/7 while the chances that they are a librarian are 2/7. The calculation is illustrated in Table 8.

	Teacher	Librarian	Total
Shy	5	2	7
Not Shy	93	0	93
Total	98	2	100

Table 8—Base rate fallacy in the ratio of shy teachers to shy librarians

The **base rate fallacy** is the tendency to ignore the base rate of a sub-population among the general population, and to focus too much attention on individuating information and less on the frequency of it occurring in the population. Say we ask, "What is more likely, that the tallest person in the world is Chinese or a Bedouin man from the small city of Rahat?" Most people will answer correctly that the man is Chinese. But say we ask, "What is more likely, that someone named Muhammad is Chinese or a Bedouin man from the city of Rahat?" Most people will wrongly answer that the man is probably Bedouin and from the city of Rahat, despite its population of only 44,000 inhabitants, and will ignore the fact that 18 million Muslims live in China.

John Smith is an American who reaches a height of 7.15 feet. What is more likely: A) John is a basketball player; B) John plays piano; or C) John is a basketball player who plays piano?

Most people respond that the probability in descending order is A-C-B, meaning that it is more likely that he is a basketball player as well as a piano player rather than just a piano player. The explanation is clear: If he is so tall, he is likely a basketball player...

One of Tversky and Kahneman's famous experiments is called "The Linda Problem." People were given the following description: Linda is 31 years old, single, outspoken, and very bright. She majored in philosophy. As a student, she was deeply concerned with issues of discrimination and social justice and also participated in anti-nuclear demonstrations. Which of the following two statements is more likely: A) Linda is a bank teller; B) Linda is a bank teller and is active in the feminist movement.

85% of the subjects chose B as the option most likely to be true.

In both of the above examples, most people chose the option that contains more conditions. The mistake in both cases, called the **conjunction fallacy**, is that it cannot be more likely that two things occur simultaneously than if only one of them occurred. If Linda is a bank teller who is active in the feminist movement, she is also a bank teller. All feminist bank tellers are bank tellers. There are more bank tellers than feminist bank tellers, therefore, it is more probable that Linda is a bank teller, feminist or not, than a feminist bank teller. I'll demonstrate this further using two circles. In the example on the right, the external circle symbolizes all the bank tellers and the internal circle indicates all the bank tellers that are also feminists. The odds of landing in the internal circle must be lower than that of ending up in the external circle. In the example on the left, the circle on the right represents a group of piano players, and the circle on the left a group of basketball players, while the dark area in the middle must represent the group of piano players that are also basketball players. The dark area must be smaller than each of the circles that formed it, and therefore, the chances of being a piano player who is also a basketball player must be smaller than the chances of being a piano player alone, even when speaking about a 7.15 foot tall American.

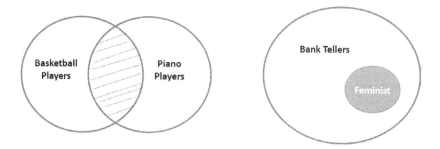

Figure 3—Illustration of the **conjunction fallacy**

Maya Bar-Hillel from The Hebrew University of Jerusalem and Efrat Neter from the Ruppin Academic Center asked subjects of a particular experiment the following question, "After completing her college studies, Sarah embarked on a trip around the world, and she described her experiences in the many letters that she sent home. One of the letters included the following description, 'I am currently in such a clean place that one could eat off the ground. Snow-covered hills are visible from the wooden cabin I am staying in, and all of the windows are decorated with colorful geranium flowers.' Where do you think Sarah wrote this letter from?"

The subjects were given a few options, and among there were "Europe" and "Switzerland." More people chose Switzerland over Europe as the place where the letter was written, even though Switzerland is in Europe.

I once asked my students how many incidents of violent crimes take place in New York City each year. On another occasion, I asked them how many violent crimes take place in New York State each year. Most people estimated that there were more violent crimes in New York City than there were in the entire state.

Unfortunately, New York City makes the headlines because of the many violent incidents that occur there, while New York State connotes green forests and flowing rivers. It seems that time and again, the stubborn rules of statistical probabilities don't work like the rules of a wild and free imagination.

A statistics joke to conclude the chapter: A statistician arrives at an airport with a bomb. After this is discovered and he is interrogated by security, he defends himself by saying that if the probability of boarding a plane with one bomb is one in a thousand, the chances of two bombs being brought onto a plane are one in a million, which is why he brought a bomb with him—he significantly lowered the odds of there being a bomb on the plane.

Conclusions:

1. When we evaluate a probability or prevalence of something occurring, we must take into account the frequency of the particular event among the population. Even though all of the inhabitants in Rahat are Muslim and only 1.5% of the inhabitants in China are Muslim, before answering the question of whether it's more likely that someone named Muhammad is from the small village of Rahat or from China, one should first check how many Muslims live in Rahat and how many live in China.

2. The probability of more than one thing taking place concurrently will always be lower than the probability of only one of those things taking place.

3. It is more likely to find a specific incident occurring within a large group than it is to find it in one of its subgroups. It is more likely that someone is a good driver than they are a taxi driver, simply because there are a great deal of drivers and not that many taxi drivers.

8

The Movie is Not as Good as the Book

"So, how was the movie *Harry Potter*?"

"It wasn't bad, but the book is a lot better."

"And how was the movie *Rocky 2*?"

"Not bad, but *Rocky 1* was a lot better."

How is it that most movies are not as good as the books upon which they are based, and how is it that most movie sequels are not as good as the first movie?

These are two examples of the phenomenon called **regression toward the mean**, which expresses the fact that after an extreme sample point is observed, there is a high probability that the following point will be closer to average.

Imagine that two people enter a room. The first person is 6.7 feet tall. Is it more likely that the second person is taller than the first, or shorter?

Imagine that the first man is 4.9 feet tall. Is it more likely that the second person is taller than the first, or shorter?

Of course, the answer to the first question is that the second person will most likely be shorter than the first, and the second answer would be that the first person is shorter than the second. Similarly, after experiencing extreme success, a more moderate success is expected to follow, and after experiencing a resounding failure, a more neutral failure is expected to follow. It is very likely that after a 6:0 win in a soccer league game, the next game is expected to have more average results. Figure 4 illustrates this further. If a certain observation lands where the arrow is pointing—for example, someone who is 6.7 feet tall—the probability that the next observation will be shorter than the first—meaning, that the second person will be shorter than 6.7 feet—is represented by the entire graph area left of the arrow, an area equaling roughly 99%, and the probability that the next person is taller than 6.7 feet makes up only 1%.

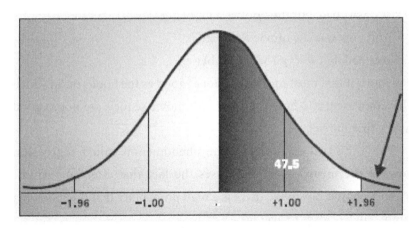

Figure 4—Normal distribution curve and regression toward the mean

How is this related to the *Harry Potter* movie? The *Harry Potter* book was a huge success. The movie is compared with the book which was met with extreme popularity, and it is difficult competing with such a hit. It's not that the movie wasn't good, it's just that the book was so successful. Books that aren't popular generally aren't used as a base for film. *Rocky 2* wouldn't have even been made if *Rocky 1* was a failure.

And since *Rocky 1* was so successful, *Rocky 2* had a very small chance of being better.

Examples of **regression toward the mean** can be found in all areas of life. In the year 2000, the Israeli police proudly announced that they had succeeded in reducing the amount of domestic violence cases. The data was impressive: The number of cases of women murdered by their partners, which rose dramatically from 11 cases in 1995 to 16 cases in 1997, returned to its original count, and in 1999, the number of similar cases went down to only 10. This was certainly an impressive feat for the Israeli police and the Israeli citizens in general.

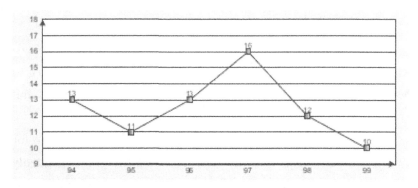

Figure 5—Distribution of cases of murdered women in Israel

In Figure 5, one can see that the number of cases of women murdered by their partners ranged from 10 to 16 between 1994 and 1999, and that on average, 12.5 such cases occurred each year. Does this indicate that the police failed during the years 1995–1997 and that the police succeeded during 1997–1999? The answer is obviously no.

The number of murder cases randomly rose in 1997 to an extreme and frightening number of 16 cases. This is indeed a very extreme situation, a rise of nearly 50% compared with the two prior years. So, what should we expect to see following such an extreme peak? A return to the average. It wasn't the police force's lack of action that led to the rise in crime and neither was it their efficiency that led to the fall. This was pure coincidence.

After a lengthy discussion among the top echelon of the Ministry of Education of a certain country, it was decided that excelling students would no longer receive positive reinforcements. This important pedagogical decision was made after it was discovered that students who improved in their studies and received positive reinforcement subsequently did worse in their studies, while students who received negative feedback reacted positively to the criticism and improved in their accomplishments. The Minister of Education was proud of this education reform.

When does a student get praised? When she improves in their studies. And what is expected to occur next? The student will return to her average performance level, but not because she was praised, but because her last results positively digressed from their average.

When does a student get scolded and his parents get called in for a motivational speech with the advisor? When her grades suddenly plummet. What is expected to occur next? The student will regress toward her average again, not because she was scolded, but because her last results negatively digressed from their average.

On Saturday, October 9, 1999, a horrible car accident took place on Highway 65 in the Galilee in Israel. A bus with 53 people inside slid on the road, flipped, and rolled into a chasm. 17 people died and the rest were injured. In light of the accident, the road was partially reconstructed—the white line was redrawn and safety railings were added. The number of traffic accident deaths on Highway 65 has been considerably low since the accident.

Can the Ministry of Transportation claim that the construction led to the reduction in traffic accident deaths since 1999? It can claim this, but the only serious explanation for the lower number of deaths from traffic accidents on Highway 65 is due the large number of deaths that occurred from that one accident, a number which can only be followed by a drop.

One basketball coach forbade the star players to be interviewed following a win. He claimed that when players get interviewed for TV following a game they excelled in, they performed worse in their next game, so it was worth refraining from being interviewed.

In a way, the coach is right. Players who get interviewed for TV after a game that went well for them generally do worse the next game. But the coach's mistake was that the drop in performance did not stem from the TV interview, but rather from the fact that the interview took place after a game where the player stood out as exceptional, and the player simply returned to his average performance level during the next game.

In general, a result will most likely be higher following an extremely low result, and vice versa.

Conclusions:

1. After yielding extreme results in a sample phenomenon, a more moderate result will generally follow. Therefore, one should be wary of the feeling of suddenly improving after a big failure or experiencing a failure after a great success.

2. Almost every phenomenon and behavior contain both random and learned components. Some student's grades could go up or down for random reasons, such as the difficulty of the test and their ability to focus, but also because the student studied more and was more prepared for the test. The number of deaths from a traffic accident in a certain part of the road is influenced by

random events, such as an oil stain on the road, but also because safety railings were or were not added to the road.

3. We have the tendency to overstate the importance of the logical component, connecting one phenomenon to another, and underestimate the importance of the random component.

4. A distinction should be made between trends and randomness. A trend is, for example, a consistent decrease in the number of deaths from traffic accidents over a long period of time in a clear direction. Randomness is, for example, an incidental decrease in the number of deaths from traffic accidents over two or three years.

5. It is worth listening, with a grain of salt, to people who interpret random events as trends, e.g., "The decrease in number of rockets fired at Israel stems from an intense hit on Hamas infrastructure." But at the same time, it could also be that one of the rocket launcher's sons got sick and the devoted father is sitting by his bedside at the hospital.

6. When the starting point is a good one (a well-made book or movie), there is a high probability that the accomplishment can't be achieved again or surpassed, and the results of a repeated attempt will not be as good.

7. Staying at the top is a lot harder than climbing there, because one can only go down from the top. In many cases, a fall occurs after a great accomplishment, because in order not to fall from a high point, one must break a new record or at least maintain the plateau.

PART II

OVERCONFIDENCE, AMBIGUITY, AND CERTAINTY

1

Chances are Low that We Understood Each Other

When I tell someone, "I am almost certain that I will call you tomorrow with an answer," what are the odds that I will actually call them tomorrow? Does "almost certain" mean 80%? 60%? Maybe just 40%?

People tend to err in their estimation of what they believe the odds are that the other person had in mind.

Try it yourselves. Write your estimations in percentages (0–100%) next to each of the following expressions.

Phrase	%(0-100)
Almost Certain	%
Good Chance	%
No Doubt	%
Probably	%
No Chance	%
Frequently	%
Expected	%
Low Probability	%

Table 8—Convert Phrases to Numerical Numbers (%)

Once you have finished writing down your estimations, copy the column with your answers to the table on page 258 and compare your answers with the numbers listed in the table. If you find that your numbers are consistently close to the minimum, you are probably a little pessimistic. If you are close to the maximum, you are probably naturally optimistic.

The well-known example in this subject is, "There's a small chance a war will break out." This is the expression that the chief of intelligence said to the Prime Minister of Israel, Golda Meir, about the likelihood that the Yom Kippur War would happen in 1973.

Thirty-three years after the war, in an interview for the *Haaretz* newspaper, Brigadier General Aryeh Shalev, who served as head of research in the Israeli Military Intelligence, said, "When I said 'small chance,' I meant less than 50%."

Golda apparently understood "small chance" to mean close to zero, and didn't call in the reserves for backup. The rest is known. There were more than 2,600 Israeli soldiers (and about 20,000 Arab soldiers) killed.

On April 30, 2001, the newspaper *Maariv* published excerpts from the State Comptroller's report, who at the time was the retired Supreme Court Justice Eliezer Goldberg. One of the paragraphs stated, "The report indicates that there is a high chance that sooner or later an earthquake will erupt with substantial intensity." This is certainly an informative sentence... Does "high chance" mean above 90% or above 5%? Does "sooner or later" refer to a few months or thousands of years? Does "substantial intensity" mean claiming the lives of thousands of victims or causing the collapse of a few old houses?

But it's not just senior officers and retired judges who make mistakes when delivering verbal probability assessments. When a type of medicine is described as having "a certain chance of not being effective," around 90% of doctors recommend it. However, when its effects are described as "quite uncertain," only around 30% of doctors recommend it. What is the difference between the two descriptions? The first one sounds positive and thus earned a high grade, while the second sounds negative and thus earned a low grade. In actuality, they pretty much say the same thing.

Years ago, I taught a course on decision theory to the department heads of a large hospital. They were asked to quantify the expression "There is a good chance." Some of the senior doctors wrote 30%–40% and others wrote 80%–90%. The doctors who gave the higher estimations asked the others, "You call a 30%–40% recovery rate 'a good chance'?"

I didn't know then what these doctors specialized in, but it turns out that for oncologists, 30%–40% are good odds, while for ear, nose, and throat doctors, 80%–90% are good odds.

Probability expressions must be estimated within the context they were uttered.

Another example touching on verbal probability expressions can be found in an excerpt of an article written in an Israeli newspaper. It said:

US intelligence sources:

30 percent chance of military clash

In the US administration, there is growing concern about the escalation of hostilities between Israel and Syria.

According to US intelligence sources, there is a 30 percent chance of a military clash occurring between Israel and Syria.
US evaluators divided the risks of escalation between Israel and Syria into three levels:

- High probability of escalation in the security zone in southern Lebanon.

- Lower probability, but still a fairly high level of risk, of a local flare-up in the Golan Heights.

- Low level of probability, but on an upward trend, of a broad military clash between Israel and Syria.

The excerpt is about evaluating United States intelligence sources regarding the prospect of a war erupting between Israel and Syria or Lebanon at the end of 1996.

The beginning looks promising: 30% chance of war. This much is clear. But upon reading the actual article, it is apparent that the Americans don't even have a rough idea of what will happen in Northern Israel.

In an interview 25 years after the Israeli Air Force bombed Iraq's nuclear reactor, the commander at the time, Lieutenant General David Ivry, said, "One of the most difficult things to do is to assess the level of risk. I told the cabinet members that there was a 'war risk level.' I then realized that I should lower the tension in the political echelon, and then the idea came to me that the risk of an attack is like the risk of the long-distance air raids deep in Egypt—1.1%. For every 100 raids, we lost one airplane. It was easier for me as well once I phrased it this way."

This is an excellent example of an expert giving a probability estimate to the deciding rank. At first, he refrained from providing a numerical assessment, but after being required to be more precise, he gave an assessment based on his past experience and his professional evaluation of the operation.

General Ivry could have, and perhaps wanted to, answer the question regarding the degree of risk of attacking the Iraqi reactor in a vague manner. A vague answer such as "faint chance" or "low risk" would provide ambiguity and serve as a protective excuse in case of failure. But the members of the cabinet found it difficult to come to a decision without a clear numerical estimate. Only a straight-forward and unambiguous numerical assessment is what enabled a rational and well-founded decision to be made.

As we all know, the Canadian military is facing extraordinary military missions whose failure could undermine national security. At any moment, a large white bear may infiltrate a military camp, or the stock of goggles against the glare of snow may not be enough for current combat unit needs.

Perhaps this is why the Canadian military is the only army to have issued clear instructions on how to translate phrases of textual uncertainty into numerical values. These guidelines are shown in Table 9 below.

Verbal Expression	Probability
Will/Is certain	[10/10]
Almost certain/extremely likely	[9/10]
Highly likely/very likely	[8/10]
Likely/probable, probably	[7/10]
slightly greater than even chance	[6/10]
even chance	[5/10]
slightly less than even chance	[4/10]
(only a) low probability/probably not	[3/10]
very unlikely/highly unlikely/extremely unlikely/little prospect	[1/10]
no prospect/will not	[0/10]

Table 9—Canadian Army guidelines for translating probability expressions

Conclusions:

1. Verbal probability assessments have the potential to protect the assessor from the need to be accurate, but it also prevents important information from reaching the decision maker.

2. A probability estimate provided using numerical values or in percentages may be clearer to the recipient. If given based on past experience and using professional knowledge and consideration of the existing reality, it can facilitate decision making.

3. When people give a verbal probability assessment, they may mean something very different from what we understand.

4. When a doctor, lawyer, or any other consultant provides us with a verbal assessment, we should press them to provide us with a numerical assessment as well.

5. The terms that describe verbal probability assessments can be interpreted subjectively, depending on the context and field in question. Sometimes, "There's a good chance" can mean 20% and sometimes it can mean 90%.

6. Verbal probability terms that sound positive are valued by listeners at a higher rate than terms that sound negative: "A certain chance" of being saved will be valued as a higher chance than a "quite uncertain" chance, although the meanings of the two expressions are similar.

7. When we provide a verbal probability estimate, we should include a numerical range: "It seems that there is a good chance that we will succeed in winning the lawsuit. I estimate that the chances are 80%–90%."

2

Most Drivers Believe they are Above Average

Most people believe, and with the utmost confidence, that they are better than others in many fields. Two thirds of lawyers believe that the side they are representing will win the cases; most entrepreneurs believe that their new business has a 70% chance at success, and that a similar business run by others has only a 40% chance.

I once asked my students to write down the percentage of students that will score higher than them in my course on decision theory. From among 80 students, only two of them recorded a number higher than 50%. Most of the students thought that their grade would be higher than the class average (or median). If everyone is above average, who is below?

Later on, I also asked the students to write down an estimate of how many Israeli drivers are better drivers than them. Here too, most of the students believed themselves to be above average.

At portfolio management conferences, participants are asked how much money they will have left at the time of their retirement, and how much other participants at the conference will have. On average, people estimated that they would be left with 5 million dollars, and that other participants would only be left with 2.5 million. Regardless of the target audience, a ratio of 2:1 was found to be very common in personal estimations compared to that of colleagues. Unfortunately, the **overconfidence effect** doesn't weaken as people become more professional, but only gets stronger.

Now let us test your degree of **overconfidence**. Table 10 presents 20 questions. Each question has two answer choices (recorded alphabetically)—one is correct and one is wrong. You are asked to circle the correct answer from among the two, and then to record the probability that you think your answer is correct in the rightmost column. The latter must be between 50%–100%. If you are certain of your answer, write down 100%. Please answer all the questions, even if you have no idea what the correct answer is. In such a case, take a guess and write down 50%.

Question	Answer A	Answer B	50-100%
The formal language of the USA is	English	Russian	100
The name of the 2nd daughter of the mayor of Beijing is	Dong	Wong	50
The population of which country is larger?	Nepal	Vietnam	90
The population of which country is larger?	Russia	USA	70
The Capital of USA is?	New York	Washington	
Population of Indonesia is?	40M	240M	
The "Magic Flute" was composed by	Mozart	Tchaikovsky	
The distance between London and Paris (km)	350	750	
Tegucigalpa is the Capital of	Honduras	Turkmenistan	

Which Book of the Old Testament has more chapters?	Isaiah	Isaiah	
Number of commercial flights per day in the USA	30000	9000	
The Capital of Morocco is?	Casablanca	Rabat	
The Currency of Nepal is?	Lempira	Rupee	
The "Beatles" were from	England	USA	
Number of babies born per day around the world	73000	370000	
Potatoes are native of	Ireland	Peru	
Out of 2300 snakes number of poisonous is?	400	300	
Population of Iceland is?	350000	2.8M	
In the USA more people die of	Diabetes	Homicide	
The chance of contracting AIDS in 1 unprotected heterosexual episode from a partner who has Aids is	0.2%	38%	
Majority of Cocoa production is in	Africa	South America	
Which country produces more rice	India	Japan	
Which country has more policemen/1000 people	India	India	
Number of Muslims in the world	700M	2.1B	

Table 10—Estimating the overconfidence effect

Once finished, calculate the average of the numbers listed in the right column and record the number you get next to the X = ___%.

Go to page 258 and check your answers. Count how many questions you got right and multiply that number by 5 to determine your rate of correct answers. Record this number as Y.

Now divide the X value by the Y value (X/Y). For example, if X, the average estimate of your confidence level is 80%, and the Y value, your actual success rate, is 70%, the result is X/Y = 80/70 = 1.14.

Understandably, measurements of character cannot be attained merely from 20 questions, and therefore the following should be treated with a great deal of skepticism: if the results you reached are above 1.3, you probably have a high level of overconfidence. If the number ranges between 1.1–1.3, you may have a certain level of overconfidence, and if the number is between 0.9–1.1, you are calibrated quite well. If your result is lower than 0.8, you probably have a serious lack of confidence.

Overconfidence plays into optimism as well. Most people see themselves through rose-colored glasses. They believe that their future is rosier than that of other people, that they are better than others when it comes to most social traits, and that they can influence and even control situations that are realistically dependent upon luck. People generally consider successes to be the fruit of their talents, and failures to be a result of bad luck. This phenomenon is called **attribution bias**. The fusion of optimism and overconfidence leads people to overestimate their knowledge and their ability to control a situation, while underestimating the risk involved in their actions.

There is an alternative idea which claims that people are actually naturally pessimistic or believe that unfavorable events have a higher chance of taking place compared with good or neutral events. Risen & Gilovich (2007) told people the following story:

> You bought a ticket for the student lottery for $5. The winning ticket gets $1,000. On the day of the lottery, you see that you forgot to bring money with you, and you are very hungry and want to buy something to eat. The student running the lottery is willing to give you the money back for your ticket.

Study participants were divided into four groups, and each group received one of the following scenarios:

1. You decide not to give the ticket back, and to find someone to borrow money from for food.
2. You exchange the ticket for money, and it is later sold to a good friend of yours.
3. You exchange the ticket for money, and it is later sold to a student you don't know.
4. You exchange the ticket for money, and it is later sold to a student whom you particularly dislike.

What are the chances that the ticket will win the lottery?

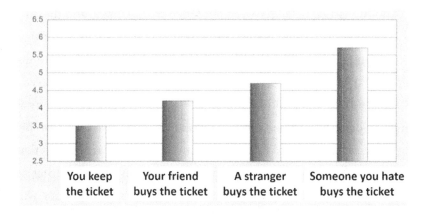

Figure 6—Pessimism and its influence on estimating odds

Similarly, researchers have found that students who didn't do their homework believed that the teacher would be more likely to call on them than on another student who didn't do their homework, and that when they did do their homework, the teacher would be more likely to call on someone else.

These two phenomena, where high probability assessments are assigned to negative outcomes, are called the **negativity bias**.

The **negativity bias** derives from the fusion of two factors: The first factor is that attention is automatically averted towards the negative result, and the other factor is that thinking about a particular phenomenon raises the odds of it occurring in the eyes of the thinker. Therefore, when it comes to results that are out of our control, negative results are often perceived as having a higher probability of occurring.

What does this say about us? Even though we are generally optimistic, at times, with negative or frightening matters—such as a plane crash or our favored sports team taking a loss—the mere thought of the negative results raises in our minds the probability that something bad will indeed occur.

Another issue related to overconfidence are the inside and the outside views of forecasts: the way in which we estimate a chance that something will happen. What is the probability that we will get a divorce? What are the chances that the startup we founded will succeed?

Most people, when estimating odds, act according to their internal view. A forecast based on someone's internal view is focused on his particular case, while taking into account the particular features that come with this case, its outline, and the obstacles expected to arise from it. When two people get married, they are sure that they will never get a divorce. They look at themselves, at how much they love each other, how good the relationship is for them, and they don't think about the divorce statistics.

A forecast that is based on an external view, however, focuses on statistics of similar problems and not of that particular case. What percentage of currently married couples will get divorced? Not necessarily looking at me and the love of my life, but at all couples. The outside view generally provides a more realistic forecast, and despite this, the inside view is very clearly preferred when intuitive forecasts are made. Sometimes, the external evaluation is knowingly and aggressively denied. When a mom tells her daughter to sign a prenuptial agreement with her impoverished fiancé, she is employing her external evaluation. When the daughter refuses, she is employing her internal evaluation.

Conclusions:

1. We have excessive self-confidence: We think that we know more than we actually do, evaluate too little information, ask the wrong questions, and don't think critically.
1. We believe that we are better than others and are right more often than others. This is why we get into legal battles and wars that could have been avoided.
2. "It won't happen to me." We believe that what applies to the entire population doesn't apply to us: We're better drivers; we won't lose in the stock market.
3. Excessive self-confidence, giving ourselves higher assessments over others, and believing that it won't happen to us often causes us to be too optimistic.
4. There are situations where it is better to be pessimistic and hesitant than to feel complete confidence. In contrast, there are situations where it is better to be optimistic and feel complete confidence than to hesitate. For example, it is best to be pessimistic and hesitant up until the decision-making stage, but to be optimistic and confident after making the decision.
5. We look at things from an internal, personal, and subjective outlook and not from an external and statistical perspective. It is worthwhile evaluating the odds using statistics as well and not only based on personal assessments. There is a certain level of

arrogance (and often foolishness) in the belief that we are fundamentally different from the rest of the population.

6. The phenomenon of self-glorification is not only related to speculations and forecasts. It exists even after the fact—we have a tendency to attribute successes to ourselves and to impose failures unto others.

7. We often suffer from self-serving bias, which means that we think the soccer team we root for has a higher chance of winning the game than the other team, and the fans of the opposing team believe the same.

3

Sooner or Later

Which song has a higher chance of winning first place in the Eurovision tournament—the first, middle, or last?

Which situation is better for a defendant—that the prosecutor speaks first and presents the accusations, or that the defense attorney first addresses the court and explains how it isn't possible that the defendant committed the crime?

We already know the importance of a first impression. It has been claimed that people make their decision about someone within the first three seconds of meeting someone new. Research in the field of emotional intelligence has brought to our attention that this process takes merely a few milliseconds.

According to one of the first studies conducted on first impressions in 1946, a job candidate described as "smart, ethical, impulsive, critical, stubborn, and jealous" was regarded higher than one described as "jealous, stubborn, critical, impulsive, ethical, and smart."

In a study following the Ohio elections in 1992, it was found that when voters searched for reasons to choose one candidate over another—a decision based on preference—they tended to vote for candidates whose names featured first on the list. But when voters sought reasons to not vote for a certain candidate—a decision based on omission—they tended to vote for candidates that were on the bottom of the list.

Essentially, two claims are being put forth here which both contradict and complement each other at the same time: According to the **primacy effect**, information presented first holds more weight than information presented in the middle. According to the **recency effect**, information presented last holds more weight than information presented in the middle.

In long-running discussions, such as legal hearings lasting several months, the more time goes by between early and later information, the weaker the **primacy effect** and the stronger the **recency effect**. This can be seen in Figure 7:

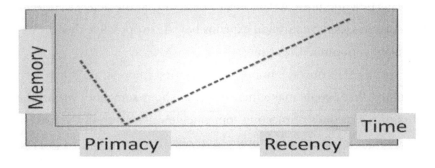

Figure 7—The effect of primacy and recency on memory

An example of the **recency effect** can be found in basketball where the coach is more affected by events (shots made) that occurred recently, in the last few minutes of the game, and less so from events that took place at an earlier time in the game or in the entire season.

Ido Erev, from the Israel Institute of Technology, and his colleagues conducted multiple studies on the matter of decisions made based on experience in the field as opposed to decisions made based on previously-known statistical data. They discovered that when it comes to repeated decisions based on experience, we generally rely on a sample size too small for making decisions, and particularly rely on information that was last received. This phenomenon was already explained in the first chapter, when the "law of small numbers" and the "hot-hand fallacy" of basketball were mentioned.

Doctors forming opinions on particular treatments will be more taken by the recent effects of treatment on their patients and less on earlier results. In a similar manner, stock exchange investors will exaggerate the weight they attribute to the behavior of a particular stock in recent times and ignore its behavior a year earlier.

In one of their articles, Ido Erev and Greg Barron provided a nice example for the recency effect and for the use of a small sample: Some car manufacturers provide consumers with the option of purchasing detachable radios. If the radio does get removed upon leaving the vehicle, the odds of it being stolen are reduced. Quite a few people have purchased removable radios, and kept pulling them out for a week or two. Eventually they got sick of removing it all the time and only then was it stolen. So what happened there?

The car dealer managed to intimidate the buyer by explaining that there were burglaries of car radios and the buyer was convinced and purchased a detachable radio. The fear subsided after a few days, and the fact that the car had not been broken into inflated the buyer's sense of security and created an impression that the odds of the radio getting stolen are lower than official statistics predicted.

Similarly, people who live in places under threat of terrorist attacks, such as the residents of cities near the border of the Gaza Strip, tend to estimate their chances of being harmed as lower than those living outside the area, say, people in Tel Aviv. How come?

This is because the inhabitants of settlements near the border, even though their traumas are still fresh in mind, live from day to day basing their estimation of a chance of a terrorist attack happening on what has happened recently in their city. Tel Aviv residents are more affected by the difficult events that transpire which the media tends to emphasize and intensify, and are therefore much more afraid than the local residents.

Daniel Kahneman found that people involved in some sort of experience are generally affected by the peak moment (the most extreme, for better or worse) of that experience, and by the emotional state they were in at the end, while the duration of the experience as a whole has nearly zero effect on the memory of pain or joy. He called it **the peak–end rule**.

This rule was proven using different means, beginning with a pain test in which hands were inserted into extremely cold water for one minute that was heated up towards the end, or listening to particularly loud music that lowered in volume towards the end. There was also data regarding patients who had undergone a colonoscopy, in which a thin tube with a camera is inserted into the body to locate malignant intestinal polyps. Patients who had the tube left in for longer and had it removed gradually reported having a better experience than those who had the tube pulled out all at once. And after dental treatment, we mostly remember the most painful moment (the injection) and the pain or partial anesthesia we felt at the end of the treatment.

In contrast, when a prisoner is about to finish his sentence, his mood begins to improve: by the end of his sentence, the prisoner goes out more during leisure time and participates in extensive rehabilitation activities. So it could be for this reason (the peak-end rule) that the painful memory of imprisonment may dim, and its effectiveness as a deterrent will weaken.

Conclusions:

1. If we want to highlight certain information during a conversation with someone else, we should make sure that the information is mentioned in the beginning or at the end of the conversation. Either way, do not let that information get lost during the conversation.

2. When choosing something, such as a new vehicle, election candidate, or spouse, we should be careful not to decide upon one specific prospect simply because it or its disadvantages were easier to remember.

3. When meeting someone new for the first time, it's worth remembering that is difficult for us to erase a bad impression that might form in that person's mind if we arrive late. They probably won't have patience and wouldn't want to hear the great excuse for our tardiness.

4. If the memory of a great vacation is mostly influenced by the most enjoyable moment of the trip and our feeling when it was all over, and less about the duration of the trip, perhaps it's better to take relatively short trips with one notable experience that ends with a business-class flight and a limousine. (Rather than taking long and tedious trips where we avoid overspending and dread the long flight back.)

4

I'd Rather Not Know

If there was a phone number to call where you could punch in the digits of your ID number and learn the date of your death, would you call that number? I wouldn't. I would rather not know. That way I can imagine that I have a whole lot more years to live. This phenomenon is called **ambiguity preference**.

What defines a firing squad? That there is more than one shooter and that some of them are shooting blanks. The shooters are aware that some of them are given empty cartridges but do not know who will receive them. What is the reason? If there was only one shooter who had real bullets, he would know for sure whether he killed the traitor. But as soon as there are a few shooters, some of whom receive fake bullets, each one of them is likely to believe that perhaps they aren't the one who shot the person.

Do we always prefer ambiguity over clarity? Not always. When it comes to receiving positive results, we actually most of the time prefer clear odds over ambiguous ones.

Daniel Ellsberg's research was the first in this field. He asked people the following question:

Consider a jug with 90 balls. Of all the balls in the jug, 30 of them are red and the rest are black and green. You must choose between black and red and then pull one ball out of the jar. If the color of the ball is identical to the one you chose, you win $1,000. Which color will you choose?

Those who choose red (A) know that the chance of them winning is 1/3. Those who choose black (B) do not know exactly what the odds are, only that they fluctuate between 0 and 2/3, or 1/3 on average as in A.

Color	Amount	Prize A	Prize B
Red	30	1000	0
Black	X	0	1000
Green	X-60	0	0
Color	**Amount**	**Prize C**	**Prize D**
Red	30	0	1000
Black	X	1000	0
Green	X-60	1000	1000

Table 11—Ellsberg's paradox and ambiguity aversion

Most people (72%) chose option A, meaning they preferred the known odds of the red ball (1/3) over the odds of the black ball (0–2/3).

In the second phase of the study, Ellsberg changed the question and said: Pull out one ball again but this time, you choose between winning with a black or green ball (C) and winning with a red or green ball (D).

Those who chose option C know that their chances of winning the prize are 2/3, while those who chose option D know that their chances of winning are between 1/3 and 1, or 2/3 on average as in C.

Most people (74%) chose option C, meaning, they preferred the known odds of the black and green balls over option D with the unclear chance. In both cases, most people preferred the clear odds over the vague odds.

Choosing A and C is irrational (according to the old rules of rationality). Those who prefer A over B act as though they believe there are more red balls than black, while those who prefer C over D act as though they believe there are more black balls than red.

People who choose A and C act as though they believe there are more red balls than black and also more black balls than red. Such an action is usually defined as irrational, but it is actually an example of **ambiguity aversion**, which means preferring clear chances over vague ones when it comes to positive results, and in this case, receiving awards.

Yoav Ganzach from Tel Aviv University examined a similar phenomenon. He found that Israeli investors prefer to invest in a well-known stock exchange, such as the Tel Aviv Stock Exchange and possibly New York, but less so in very profitable but distant and exotic stock exchanges such as those of China or India. This phenomenon is called the **mere exposure effect**.

But what happens regarding negative results? Ilan Yaniv, Debbie Benador, and Michal Sagi from the Hebrew University of Jerusalem asked students the following question:

A simple test can reveal whether someone is a carrier of genes that lead to the development of Huntington's disease—a serious illness that is only discovered at the age of 35–50. It is an incurable disease that results in death.

1. Would you want to get tested?
2. Would you want your partner to get tested?
3. Would you want your future partner to get tested?

48% of respondents did not want to be tested, 45% wanted their partner to be tested, and 65% wanted their future partner to be tested. The results indicate that many people prefer not to know about a negative phenomenon if they are unable to deal with it. In contrast, if they can deal with the problem, as in the case of leaving a future spouse, most study participants preferred knowledge over ambiguity.

In a study I co-ran with my good friend and colleague from the Ruppin Academic Center, Dr. Liema Davidovich, we asked a large group of students four questions. Some of the questions were positive (prizes, vacations, etc.) and some were negative (fines, diseases, etc.).

Here are two questionnaires. Answer the positive and negative questions yourselves and afterwards, compare your answers with the results of the study presented below after Question 4. A score of 1 expresses complete ambiguity aversion, and a score of 7 expresses complete ambiguity preference.

1a) A traveler was fined 10,000,000 won while travelling in South Korea, which is about 6,000 euros. The traveler must pay the fine within a year, but must decide today which currency to use to pay the fine—in won or in euros. Which would you choose?

7	4	1
Very likely that I would choose won	No preference	Very likely that I will choose euros

1b) A scientist won a prize from the South Korean government in the amount of 10,000,000 won, which is about 6,000 euros. The prize will be awarded in a year, but the scientist must decide today which currency to receive the prize in—won or euros. Which would you choose?

7	4	1
Very likely that I would choose won	No preference	Very likely that I will choose euros

2a) Two people traveled to Africa. Their families received an alarming message saying that the two travelers were taken to local hospitals.

One is infected with meningitis A, with a mortality rate is 30%, and the other is infected with meningitis B, with a mortality rate of 10%–50%. The travelers cannot be contacted. Which family's situation is better in your opinion?

7	4	1
The type B patient's family	No preference	The type A patient's family

2b) Two people traveled to Africa. Their families received an alarming message saying that the two travelers were taken to local hospitals. One is infected with meningitis A, with a recovery rate of 70%, and the other is infected with meningitis B, with a recovery rate of 50%–90%. The travelers cannot be contacted. Which family's situation is better in your opinion?

7	4	1
The type B patient's family	No preference	The type A patient's family

3a) An Israeli traveler and an Italian traveler were captured by a cannibalistic tribe in Papua New Guinea. The tribe is known for killing 50% of the foreigners they capture. The sacrifices are chosen via the tossing of a coin or the blowing of feathers by the local witch doctor. Even with the feather blowing method, the chances of dying are 50% on average. If you were the Israeli traveler, which method would you prefer to choose between you and the Italian as victims?

7	4	1
Very likely that I will choose the flower blowing	No preference	Very likely that I will choose the coin tossing

3b) An Israeli traveler and an Italian traveler were captured by a cannibalistic tribe in Papua New Guinea. The tribe is known for killing 50% of the foreigners they capture. The tribe is about to decide who to release. The process of selecting the hiker to be released is done by either the tossing of a coin or the blowing of feathers by the local witch doctor. Even with the feather blowing method, the chances of being released are 50% on average. If you were the Israeli traveler, which method would you want them to choose to decide who should be released—you or the Italian?

7	4	1
Very likely that I will choose the flower blowing	No preference	Very likely that I will choose the coin tossing

4a) After a month of difficult service in the reserves, a choice must be made as to which of the 90 reserve soldiers will stay another week and which will be released to go home. The lottery is done by taking a ball out of a jar. The jar has red, black, and yellow balls. There are 90 balls in total, 30 of which are red and the rest are black or yellow. As one of the reservists, you can choose whether you stay another week by taking out either a red ball or a yellow ball. Which color would you prefer to pull out?

7	4	1
Very likely that I will choose yellow	No preference	Very likely that I will choose red

4b) Out of 90 students, 30 are chosen as winners of an all-expense paid week in Europe. The lottery is done by removing a ball from a jug. The jug has red, black, and yellow balls. There are a total of 90 balls, 30 of which are red, and the rest are black or yellow. You can choose between the prize being a reward for drawing out a red ball or for drawing a yellow ball. Which color would you choose to be the reward?

7	4	1
Very likely that I will choose yellow	No preference	Very likely that I will choose red

The following are the results of the study:

The average answer for question 1a was 4.28.

The average answer for question 1b was 2.49 (very significant difference).

The average answer for question 2a was 4.52.

The average answer for question 2b was 3.74 (very significant difference).

The average answer for question 3a was 4.34.

The average answer for question 3b was 4.02 (significant difference).

The average answer for question 4a was 3.86.

The average answer for question 4b was 3.04 (very significant difference).

The results of the study clearly show that when it comes to negative outcomes, most people prefer ambiguity, whereas when it comes to positive outcomes, most people prefer lack of ambiguity. In my opinion, the reason for this is that ambiguity can be a good excuse for failure. When it comes to the negative realm, i.e., losses or troubles, it is clear to us that the result can be negative, so if the decision process is vague, we can place the blame of the fact that we did not know exactly what was going on.

Conclusions:

1. When it comes to positive outcomes like winning a cash prize or a vacation, or recovering from an illness, most people want to know the odds more clearly and reject ambiguity, meaning they prefer options where the chances are clearer and less vague.

2. When it comes to negative outcomes like financial loss, punishment, or suffering from an illness, most people prefer not to know what the odds are clearly and prefer ambiguity, i.e., they prefer options where the chances are more vague and less clear.

3. Some women avoid breast cancer testing, and some men avoid prostate cancer testing, even though early detection of the disease can increase the chances of recovery. This phenomenon of ambiguity preference can have fatal consequences.

4. Accurate information does not increase the chances of a negative event occurring. On the contrary, ignoring information for superstitious reasons or for "provoking fate" may increase the chance that the adverse event will indeed occur. On the other hand, if accurate information is of no use—a date of death, for example—it is better not to deal with it.

5. Sometimes the reason for avoiding information stems from the fact that new information may require significant change and dramatic decisions, and those who think they do not have the power to deal with the decisions prefer to avoid the information that leads to them.

5

Certainty is the End of All Hope

In reality shows like *The Voice* or *Survivor*, we experience joy when someone succeeds and moves on to the next stage. Is this feeling of joy the same in the different stages? Does someone who knows he is one of the five finalists feel very different from someone who is one of the three finalists? In the first case, the objective chances of winning the competition are 1/5, i.e., 20%, and in the second case, 1/3, i.e., 33%. Does the candidate feel the difference?

Every beer lover is aware of the difference between 1/3-liter and 1/2-liter glasses. Does this feeling also exist in the realm of probability? The emotional expressions of probabilities are hope and fear. Hope is an emotion that signifies the chance of something good taking place, and fear is an emotion that indicates the chance of something bad taking place. It turns out that these two emotions behave in a rather unique way. They are not linear or proportional, but have a convoluted shape. In Figure 8, the straight line represents rational behavior. According to this line, one can see that a probability of 20% is double the probability of 10%, and thus, a probability of 100% is double that of 50%. A straight line in mathematics always expresses a uniform pace. From the probability line, we gather that the straight line means that any 1%

change in the odds is of equal weight. A change of 1% from 32% to 33% will have the same weight as a change from 99% to 100%.

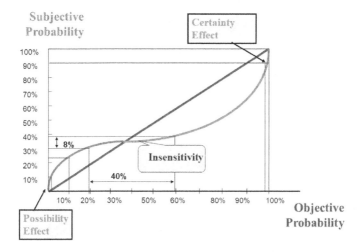

Figure 8 — The subjective-probability distribution

This is not the case in reality. Some changes of 1% bear much greater significance than other changes. This is reflected in the convoluted curve of the subjective-probability distribution. One can see that the transition from 0% to 1% is very significant. An objective change from 0% to 1% is subjectively perceived as a change of about 10%. This phenomenon is called the **possibility effect**. The transition from "uncertain" to "maybe", even if the "maybe" is only 1%, is dramatic.

A few years ago I contracted a strange skin disease, and the doctors did not know what had happened to me. After the results of all the tests came back negative, the doctor offered me a special test, one that is generally only performed at another hospital, and checked whether my symptoms are a result of cancer. The doctor reassured me that the chance of my red skin being cancer is only 1%, but she wanted to be sure it wasn't.

I remember the trip to the other hospital. I thought about my life and who would inherit my meager possessions. The chance that I would be killed in a car accident on that trip was equal to the chance that I had cancer. One small percentage that caused me extreme anxiety.

The opposing phenomenon to the **possibility effect** is the **certainty effect**. Here, much weight is given to the transition from 99% to 100%. Certainty is the end of all hope. Although the objective difference between 99% and 100% is only 1%, the subjective difference is almost 10%.

The family of a missing soldier whose whereabouts have not been known for decades knows that there is a 99% chance that he is no longer alive. But in the hearts of the family, the remaining percentage secretly evokes great hope. If his body is located and brought in for burial, the family will feel heavy, even though the soldier's captivity occurred decades ago.

I met Mickey Goldwasser, the mother of the late Udi Goldwasser, a soldier on reserve duty who was abducted and killed during a Hezbollah attack on the northern border of Israel. We met at a seminar at the Ruppin Academic Center where I teach. Mrs. Goldwasser was asked if she believed during the entire period of uncertainty that Udi was still alive. Her response made my heart stop. She told me about the "prisoner exchange" ceremony on the Lebanese border, which she watched on TV, and said, "Until the moment I saw the two caskets being removed from the Lebanese vehicles, I was certain that I would be hugging my son within a few minutes."

But certainty is not only the end of hope, it is also the end of fear. I was 99% sure that I did not have cancer, but when the medical results came in, and determined with finality that I did not have cancer—I felt extremely relieved.

The certainty effect has many implications in the economic and medical fields, and no less so in politics. Opponents of peace treaties, for example, will justly claim that there is no certainty that the enemy will honor the agreement, and thus will continue arguing—this time, unjustly—that this is a reason not to sign the treaty.

If the odds of the enemy honoring the agreement are only 90% or 80% or 50% or 10%, is it really not worth signing the peace treaty? **One who seeks and demands certainty as a condition for every deed will do nothing.** The analysis must be conducted according to the objective odds and the results, and not according to the excessive weight assigned to the difference between absolute certainty (100%) and very high odds (99%).

Maurice Allais, a Nobel Prize-winning French economist, asked the following question:

> Suppose Jar A has 100 red balls and Jar B has 89 red balls, 10 blue balls and one white ball and you put your hand inside a jar and take out one ball. If the ball is red, you get a million dollars; if it is blue, you get $5 million; and if it is white, you get nothing. Which would you prefer—to take a ball from Jar A or Jar B?

The top of Figure 9 shows the options:

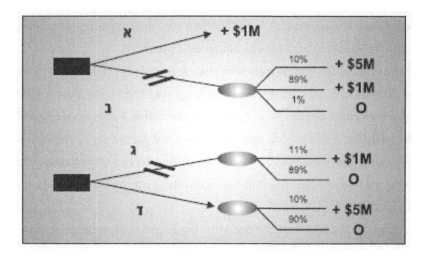

Figure 9—The Allais paradox

Most people preferred the option of taking a ball from Jar A and not Jar B. They preferred to get a certain $1 million over choosing Jar B, a lottery with a 10% chance of winning $5 million, 89% of winning $1 million, and a 1% chance of not earning anything. Maurice Allais then asked the following question:

> Jar C has 11 red balls and 89 white balls, and Jar D has 10 blue balls and 90 white balls. Reach into a jar and remove one ball. If you get a red ball, you get a million dollars; if it is blue, you get $5 million; if it is white, you get nothing. Would you prefer to remove a ball from Jar C or Jar D?

The bottom of Figure 9 shows the options. Most people preferred to take a ball from Jar D rather than Jar C. They preferred a 10% chance of winning 5 million dollars over an 11% chance of winning 1 million dollars.

If so, then what is the paradox? In the first question, there is a 100% chance of removing a red ball from Jar A and an 89% chance of removing a red ball from Jar B, meaning that the difference in terms of red balls is 11% in favor of Jar A. This difference stands against a 10% chance of winning $5 million with Jar B. But this is exactly the dilemma between pitcher C and pitcher D. Ergo, it would be rational that whoever preferred Jar A over Jar B would prefer Jar C over Jar D. The reason this does not happen is because the transition from 10% to 11% is not as impressive as the transition from 99% to 100%. The certainty effect is very strong.

A study by Israeli researchers cast some doubt on the certainty effect. The study was published in the important journal *Nature* and dealt with the comparison between bee decisions and human decisions. Contrary to the certainty effect—which states, for example, that most people would prefer receiving $3,000 with certainty over $4,000

Maurice Allais

with an 80% probability of receiving it— the researchers claimed that in nature and during human life, problems don't appear with clear cut data, and thus, estimates regarding odds are more ambiguous. Bees, for example, preferred a source of sugar which gave them a solution with a high concentration of sugar 80% of the time and distilled water 20% of the time, over a source that gave them a solution with a medium level concentration of sugar 100% of the time. It has been found that living things, most people included, will not necessarily prefer the option that is certain. They vaguely remember the successes and failures, and choose an alternative that according to their memory and experience, has led to more positive results, regardless of the degree of success each time.

Let us return to the subjective-probability curve (Figure 8). In the center of the graph, between 20% and 60%, the curve hardly rises. We see a marked insensitivity to changes in probability in the middle range. A person who might win a prize out of three potential winners feels about as much hope as the person who might win a prize out of five potential winners. An objective change of 40% between 20% and 60% is subjectively perceived as a change of only 8%.

Rottenstreich and Hsee published a charming study on the effect of emotion on the shape of the subjective-probability curve. The researchers asked study participants how much they would be willing to pay in order to avoid a lottery that had a 1% chance of losing $20, and how much they would be willing to pay to avoid a lottery that had a 1% chance of getting an electric shock (painful but not dangerous). The answers were $1 to avoid the chance of losing money and $7 to avoid the chance of an electric shock.

The researchers repeated the question, but changed the odds of losing $20 or getting an electric shock to 99% and 100% respectively. The average of the answers is given in Table 12.

Probability	$20 loss	Electric shock
1%	$1	$7
99%	$18	$10
100%	$20	$20 dollars

Table 12—What people are willing to pay in order to avoid a lottery in which they might lost $20 or get an electric shock

The results of the study seem very surprising at first glance. People are willing to pay $7 to avoid a 1% chance of an electric shock, and only $10 if the chance is 99%? Are people willing to pay less to avoid a 99%

chance of getting a painful electric shock than to avoid a 99% chance of losing $20? While the results may not seem plausible at first glance, the researchers' explanation is fascinating—the subjects' answers to the question about money behave, more or less, according to the odds. In contrast, the respondents' answers to the question of electric shock correspond, and even exaggerate, to the subjective-probability curve.

In accordance with the **possibility effect**, the first percent really scared the subjects, and thus they were willing to pay a high price to avoid the lottery. The transition from 1% to 99% had almost no effect on the perception of probability, meaning that the field of insensitivity greatly expanded, and in the end, following the **certainty effect**, the transition from 99% to 100% was dramatic and led to a doubling in payment. When it comes to emotional results such as fear, love, hate, jealousy, etc., there is a marked insensitivity to changes in probability. When we get excited about the possibility that we will win something or that we will suffer from something, we stop thinking probabilistically, and changes in the odds of the event occurring lose their meaning.

Does she love me? Such a question cannot be answered by 35% yes, 40% a little, and 25% no. The answer to this question is yes or no. Love has no percentage. When it comes to emotions, we tend to think and feel in an "all-or-nothing" manner. To illustrate a decision made out of anger and extraordinary excitement, you are invited to read the ending of Dan Lerner's murder story in my book *Decision to Kill*.

Conclusions:

1. When we are very excited, maybe it's best not to make decisions just then, but to do so at another time or to consult with someone who is more calm.

2. We stop thinking logically when we get excited. We neglect the

odds, and the question turns into "all -or-nothing" or "yes-or-no," and ceases to be a question of "there is a chance that it will be so and there is a chance that it won't."

3. We assign too much importance to the transition from a 99% chance to a 100% chance. The resoluteness and wholeness of 100% give us a sense of absolute certainty. The one percent before certainty is perceived as uncertainty, and we distort its sense of size and meaning. In exactly the same way, we assign too much importance to the transition from a 0% chance to a 1% chance.

4. Certainty is a good thing but it isn't necessary when making decisions. When it comes to most of the important life decisions, it's very hard to advance and succeed without taking calculated risks (not gambling!).

PART III

TAKING RISKS

1

Right Foot in Ice Water and Left Foot in Boiling—Is the Average Warm?

Insurance companies make a lot of money. Why do we pay them such high premiums? What do they give us for our money, and what do they have that we do not have?

The answer is that insurance companies work on averages and we do not. We are each private cases, and if our cars are stolen, we cannot say that almost no cars were stolen in our city, on average. There is no average when it comes to one particular case.

The insurance company, since it insures many cars and knows the car-theft statistics of different parts of the country, can calculate how many cars will be stolen this year with great accuracy, and charge a premium to cover the damages accordingly. At the same time, the company earns a large profit.

For example, suppose one hundred people insure their car worth $20,000 and suppose that on a multi-year average, the chances of car theft in the same area are 3% per year, meaning, about three cars. (Let us ignore the damages caused by road accidents and focus only on theft.) The insurance company will charge a premium of about $1,000 from all one hundred car owners ($100,000), will pay $20,000 to the three people whose car was stolen ($60,000), and will yield a profit of $40,000.

Even though we pay 5% for the insurance premium and the company only pays 3% in compensation, we are not able to save that 2% that makes up the difference. We pay, and pay dearly, to buy ourselves certainty.

This calculation of the mean, or as statisticians call it the **expected value**, is true when there is no risk or when the risk is low. If, for example, a cell phone costs $500 and its annual insurance cost is $200, it is definitely not worth insuring because there is almost no risk. You would lose $500, at most. Not fun but not terrible. Then which cases bear no risk and in which cases is the risk negligible? There are three situations in which there is no or almost no risk:

A. When there is complete certainty:
If I rent an apartment and the rent is in dollars, and I receive an income from an apartment I rent out that is also in dollars, and for the same amount, I have no need to insure against changes in the dollar-exchange rate. If the dollar rises, my rent will rise equally on both sides, and there is no uncertainty.

On the other hand, if someone exports products abroad and receives payment in dollars, but uses a different currency to pay for expenses in the country they live in, that person should equip themselves with exchange-rate and foreign trade-risks insurance in order to ensure their income and not risk losing money due to changes in currency rates.

B. When dealing with relatively small amounts:
In the above cell phone example, damage caused by loss of the device is not too devastating, while the price for insurance is relatively high. In such a case, we might lose the device and thus lose some money, but no

significant change will occur in our lives as a result of this minor loss.

A few years ago, my wife received an offer to insure our freezer for 3 years for the price of $240. After making sure she was not being offered life insurance for her partner, she asked me, "What do you say, should we get this insurance?" (My wife usually consults with me regarding sums smaller than $500. Beyond that, she decides on her own.)

I asked her, "How much does such a freezer cost?" The answer was about $1000. Is it worth insuring a freezer for a premium that's about 8% of its value ($80 per year for a value of $240)? If we were storing rare medicine in the freezer that requires immediate repair if it gets ruined, we would probably get the insurance. But with these freezers, there is usually just some chicken under a pile of ice. So what would we need insurance for? If the freezer breaks down, we will have it repaired. The same goes for all the many household appliances: TV, refrigerator, washing machine, dishwasher, and the like.

C. When dealing with a large number of cases or multiple repetitions: Egged, a major bus company in Israel, does not insure its buses. It has about 3,000 buses, and despite the fact that each one costs about $200,000—or maybe because of this—the company saves huge sums through self-insurance. If the bus gets damaged, the company pays to have it repaired.

Egged is such a large and powerful company that it can afford to serve as its own insurance company, which means assuming the company's risks and not paying someone else to bear the risks.

The company *Smith & Sons for the Transport of the Nation*, which owns one bus (and the owner has one son in the meantime), cannot afford to not insure the bus. In the event of an accident, the father's and son's earnings will be lost.

However, there isn't necessarily a connection between the number of vehicles the company owns and the decision whether to insure them or not. Microsoft doesn't need to insure its vehicles either, but this is due to the fact that it is a large enough company to finance damage caused to one of the vehicles and save on insurance expenses. Of course, the China Life Insurance Company does not have to insure its vehicles either.

Insurance should only be bought if the damage that may occur is so great that it could potentially undermine the insured's financial standing. Let's revisit the moving companies. A company that owns 30–50 vehicles doesn't need to insure them. Each vehicle constitutes 2%-3% of the company's value, and even if one vehicle got completely wrecked, the company would be able to continue operating almost as if nothing has changed.

Let's say you were offered to participate one time in the following lottery: A coin toss. If the coin lands on *tails*, you win $1,200, but if it lands on *heads*, you lose $1,000. Would you play?

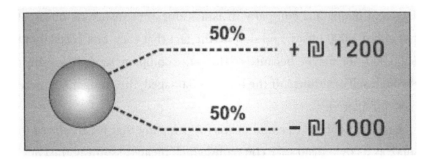

Figure 10—Lottery example

Most people I know, myself included, would not play.

And what if you could toss the coin 50 times?

Although the lottery is worth it even if the coin is tossed only once, there is a risk of losing $1,000, which is a bit unnerving and not so pleasant. However, when the lottery is offered 50 times, its mean will more or less "work", and we will earn an average of $5,000 for the coin tosses in total.

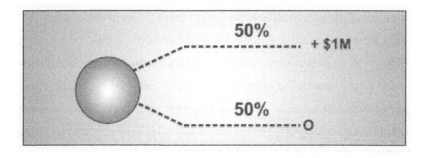

Figure 11—Lottery example

What about this next scenario: You have a lottery ticket numbered 9415867. You read in the paper that either the number 9415867 or 9415367 won a prize of 1 million dollars. The third digit from the right is blurry, making it hard to tell if it's an 8 or a 3. The odds seem equal. If the number is 8, you won a million dollars, and if it is 3, you didn't win anything.

What is the minimum amount of money for which you would be willing to sell your card?

Would you agree to sell it for less than half-a-million dollars, half-a-million dollars, or more?

Most people I know, myself included, would be willing to sell the ticket for much less than half-a-million dollars. If someone offered me $400,000 in cash, I would take it. I would also accept $300,000, and maybe even $100,000. I suspect that if I turned down an offer of $100,000 and in the end, didn't win anything from the lottery, it would irk me until the end of my days.

Such questions classify people into three groups: those who are risk averse—who would give up on uncertain transactions for an amount lower than the expected value (in this case, less than half-a-million dollars); those who are risk neutral—who would forfeit their odds for the exact amount of the expected value; and those who risk seekers, also known as "gamblers"—who would demand more than what they could have earned on average for a deal that is uncertain.

By the way, when successful executives in the United States were asked the million-dollar question I posed above, their answer, surprising for those unfamiliar with the business world, averaged between $400,000 and $450,000. They showed a low level of risk aversion, but did not gamble at all.

In business, and in life in general, risk-taking is a necessary condition for success. But taking risks is not the same as gambling. Risk-taking is an action that favors an uncertain decision with a high profit over a certain decision with a low profit. Gambling is a decision made against the odds, while taking a risk is a decision made in line with the odds.

A person who constantly succeeds probably doesn't take enough risks. If someone has been riding a horse for ten years and has never fallen off, they probably have been riding a wooden pony.

Taking risks is an integral part of life; it is the engine for growth in a carefree life and the only way out during critical situations. When there is nothing to lose, both humans and animals behave differently than usual and tend to take more risks. A study looking at birds examined bird preferences: Would a bird prefer a food source that provides three pieces of grain with a hundred percent certainty, or one that provides six pieces of grain or zero with equal odds; in both cases, the bird will receive an average of three pieces of grain.

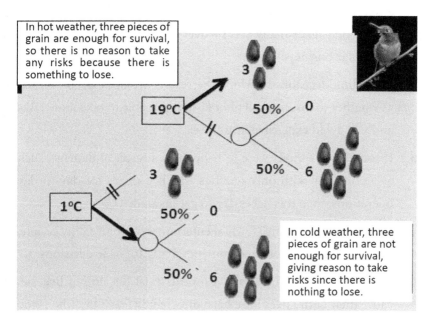

In hot weather, three pieces of grain are enough for survival, so there is no reason to take any risks because there is something to lose.

In cold weather, three pieces of grain are not enough for survival, giving reason to take risks since there is nothing to lose.

In the experiment, when the temperature was relatively high, the birds preferred the safe and reliable source of food, whereas when the temperature was very low, the birds preferred the uncertain source. This is because when the temperature is high, there is enough grain for the birds to survive, thus choosing the safest alternative. But in extreme, cold weather, the birds require six grains to survive, so the birds had no choice but to take a risk and "go all out"—they had nothing to lose. Choosing the certain option wouldn't satisfy the required need, however, while choosing the uncertain one here gives them a 50% chance of survival throughout winter.

Conclusions:

1. More risks can be taken when making decisions that are recurring and ongoing. The higher expected value will materialize in the long run. This is why, for example, one can risk more when making

a decision about which pension fund investment to choose—a matter that takes many years—over a one-time investment in a particular business.

2. Regarding decisions in which the results are not extreme—such as whether to insure a cell phone—it is possible to take more risks and still avoid expensive insurance.

3. If something serious were to happen as a result of damage, such as a company with only one bus which it needs for day-to-day operations, then it is necessary to get insured.

4. Gambling can be a nice form of entertainment for wealthy people, but it is definitely not a recommended way to make decisions.

5. "Life requires much courage. Cowards exist but do not live, because their entire lives have been directed by fear. One who is too aware of security and safety remains imprisoned in a very small corner, almost as if inside a self-built prison. He is safe but not alive. These objects really need to move toward the unknown. They must learn that there is no home. Life is a pilgrimage. There are places to park overnight but we've got to get moving again in the morning. The only thing that drives life is risk. The more you risk, the more you live."

—Osho *Life, Love, Laughter*

2

How Seatbelts Led to Drunk Driving

What is the risk? Risk perception and the decision of whether to take the risk consist of three components:

A. The probability of obtaining negative results.

B. The level of severity of the possible negative outcomes.

C. The expected benefit from the dangerous activity.

For example, do women ride motorcycles less than men because they: A) think the chance of an accident is higher than men think? B) Believe that severity of injury is worse than men believe in the event of an accident? C) Enjoy the experience of riding a motorcycle less than men?

Some people would interpret th3e minority of women motorcyclists as a result of fear—fear of there being an accident or fear of how bad the accident would be. In my opinion, women are no more afraid of motorcycles but enjoy them less. A new study states that taking risks is the manner in which males demonstrate their masculinity to females. For example, it has been found that more men than women would cross a busy road, taking a high risk, especially in the presence of women.

It's been claimed that the degree of risk taken is constant, meaning that each person has a risk level that suits him. If he reduces the risk in one way, he will increase it in another way. This phenomenon is called **risk homeostasis**.

In Canada, they found that the law enforcing the use of a seatbelt in a vehicle has raised the speed limit, and blood alcohol content in drivers. The sense of security that the belt provided the drivers allowed them to loosen the reins such that the level of risk while driving increased. Even though an extensive campaign against drunk driving helped bring about an 18% decrease in alcohol-related road accidents, it led to a 19% increase in road accidents for other reasons. Similar results were obtained in an experiment with taxi drivers in Munich after installing an ABS brake system in their vehicle, which amplified the aggression in their driving behavior. Another study showed that when cyclists wear a helmet, vehicles that pass them drive 3.5 inches closer than when they are not wearing a helmet. Drivers also tended to drive closer to male cyclists more than to female cyclists.

Similarly, the use of clever medicine bottle caps led to a decrease in parents' concern for storing medicine on top shelves. This sense of security afforded by the special lids brought about a careless attitude towards the children's safety.

Other examples leading to this behavior are sunscreen and nicotine-free cigarettes. Sunscreen with high SPF causes people to stay in the sun longer, and nicotine-free cigarettes makes smokers smoke more than when the cigarettes were full of nicotine.

Policymakers who set rules and regulations should take this human behavior into account instead of adopting regulations that seem to reduce risk, but in reality, actually increase it.

An example of this is the proposed law that pubs be closed to youth at midnight. This regulation was meant to reduce the knife fights that took place in places where the kids would gather on the weekends. But what did the legislator think the kids would do—go home and listen to Rostropovich's cello? The knife fights would just move to a different hidden location.

Another example is the United States National Prohibition Act. The 18th Amendment of the United States Constitution was enacted in 1919 and prohibited the production, transportation, and sale of liquor throughout the country. It is not for nothing that this law was repealed by the 21st Amendment of the Constitution in 1933. The enormous increase in crime which was caused as a result of this enactment over-shadowed the few benefits, if any, that resulted from it.

I also highly believe that the policies enacted today against drug users and dealers are a double-edged sword. In a system with internal homeostasis, pressure in one place can lead to relaxation in another. I would suggest using education to solve the drug and alcohol problem, in order to reduce stress throughout the entire system, and not through a law that attempts to address the problem in just one narrow sector.

Conclusions:

1. When debating whether to take a risk regarding a particular issue, we should ask ourselves: What are the odds that we will fail? How intense of a failure might it be? And why should we take the risk at all?
2. When reducing the risk in one way, we should check and see that we are not increasing it indirectly in another way.

3

Is Smoking Allowed During Prayers?

"Is it permissible to smoke while praying?" the man asked the rabbi, and was met with an absolute negative response. "Is it permissible to pray while smoking?" the man asked the rabbi, who replied, "Prayer is allowed in any situation, my son."

The rabbi's response depends on the way the question is presented to him. When the question is phrased in a positive light, it invites a different answer than when phrased in a negative light. One of the most famous studies in the field of decision theory is Kahneman and Tversky's known as the "Asian disease" problem. The study did not deal with the epidemic itself, but rather with the way in which people responded to the problem which was presented in a positive and negative light.

Imagine that the U.S. is preparing for the outbreak of an unusual Asian disease, which is expected to kill 600 people. Two alternative programs to combat the disease have been proposed. Assume that the exact scientific estimate of the consequences of the programs were as follows:

If Program A is adopted, 200 people will be saved. (72%)

If Program B is adopted, there is 1/3 probability that 600 people will be saved, and 2/3 probability that no people will be saved. (28%)

Which of the two programs would you favor?

72% of the respondents in the original study preferred Program A. The second part of the study included the same question but with different wording:

> Imagine that the U.S. is preparing for the outbreak of an unusual Asian disease, which is expected to kill 600 people. Two alternative programs to combat the disease have been proposed. Assume that the exact scientific estimate of the consequences of the programs were as follows:
>
> If Program C is adopted, 400 people will die. (22%)
>
> If Program D is adopted, there is 1/3 probability that nobody will die, and 2/3 probability that 600 people will die. (78%)
>
> Which of the two programs would you favor?

78% of the respondents preferred Program D. Even though the dry data in the two questions was identical, the results were totally opposite. In the first study, where the data was presented in a positive light, (saving lives,) subjects clearly preferred to go with the certain choice and not to take risks. People probably thought to themselves: I won't gamble or play with human life if I can save 200 people.

In the second, reworded study, in which the data was presented in a negative light, (human mortality,) there was a clear preference for uncertainty and risk taking. People probably thought to themselves: I don't want to kill 400 people. If all 600 people die, it won't be because of me. It's up to God.

The above example does a fine job illustrating **the framing effect**, i.e., the fact that alternative presentations of the data can lead to very different decisions. And this is also an example of the **reflection effect**: The two questions are sort of mirror images of each other. The first question is reflected in the second. However, when the data is presented positively, for example in the context of saving lives, financial gain, or high scores, we prefer sticking to what's certain and tend to avoid taking risks, whereas when the data is presented negatively, for example when it comes to death, financial loss, and failures, we prefer uncertainty and tend to take risks.

Here are two more examples of **the framing effect**. Two researchers in the United States asked people the following question:

A family that owns two vehicles is considering replacing one of them:

A jeep with a fuel consumption of 10 miles per gallon for a jeep with a fuel consumption of 20 miles per gallon.

1. A private car with a fuel consumption of 20 miles per gallon with a car that has a 50 miles per gallon fuel consumption.
2. Which car should be replaced in order to conserve gas?

Most of the subjects thought that it would be better to replace the private car. However, when the first question was asked in a slightly different way, the error in the answer to the first question was brought to light.

A family that owns two vehicles, each driven 100 miles a week, is considering replacing one of them:

1. A jeep that requires 10 gallons of fuel per 100 miles with a jeep that requires 5 gallons per 100 miles.
2. A private car that consumes 5 gallons of fuel per 100 miles with a car that consumes 2 gallons of fuel per 100 miles.
3. Which car should be replaced in order to conserve gas?

In the latter case, it is quite clear that replacing the jeep is the more worthwhile option. Saving five gallons a week by replacing the jeep is better than saving only three gallons on a private car.

Many years ago, my good friend, the late Professor Justen Passwell, who served as Director of the Pediatric Wards in the Tel Hashomer Hospital at the time, told me about one of his dilemmas. A baby was born at the hospital with a severe heart defect. The matter was extremely complicated. The baby girl could be operated on in Israel, but there wasn't adequate knowledge in that specific field at the time, and the doctor estimated that the chances of the operation being a success in Israel were about 20%. The operation could also be done in the United States, but the cost would be close to $150,000, and the family didn't have enough financial resources. Either way, the success of the operation in the United States was also not guaranteed, with a 40% chance of success.

The family was prepared to mortgage all of their property and move to the United States because the chances of success were double there than in Israel. I suggested that the doctor present to the family the data of the surgery in Israel and in the United States, not only in the positive light (chances of success), but also in a negative light (chances of failure); meaning, stated as the chances of failure in Israel is 80% and in the United States is 60%. The chances of success in the United States is double than in Israel, however, this does not mean that the chances of failure in Israel are double those of the United States. In addition, as I showed in a previous chapter with the subjective-probability curve, the transition from 10% to 20% seems more significant than the transition from 60% to 80%. Presenting the problem with a positive spin, which in this case meant presenting the chances of success, would most likely lead the decision maker to opt for surgery in the United States since the chances of success there were twofold. However, presenting the problem in a negative light will somewhat blur the difference between the rate of failure in Israel (80%) and the rate of failure in the United States (60%), and more attention would be given to the heavy financial costs involved in surgery abroad.

Conclusions:

1. Before making a decision, it is worth phrasing the problem at hand in different ways, alternating between positive and negative wording, and examining whether the change in phrasing also leads to a change in how one feels about the decision.

2. It's worth remembering that when problems are presented in a positive light, with emphasis on success, profit, and good things, most people will prefer the assured choice, will settle for less, and avoid uncertainty.

3. However, when problems are presented in a negative light, with emphasis on failure, loss, and bad things, most people prefer the riskier choice.

4. We have the tendency to avoid risk-taking in order to achieve a secure outcome, and on the other hand, to take risks in order to avoid a definite loss.

PART IV

SEEMINGLY
SOLID LOGIC

1

What is Certain is Certain

"Do you have fresh milk, but from today?" the man asked the waiter in the cafe.

"Absolutely," replied the waiter.

"If so," said the man, "then I will drink black coffee."

According to the **sure-thing principle**, if someone prefers Option A over Option B under certain circumstances, and still prefers Option A over Option B when the conditions are lacking, then this person will prefer Option A over Option B regardless of whether the condition is met or not.

If a person decides to take an umbrella on days when the forecast says it will rain and on days when it says it won't, this person doesn't have to wait until the end of the news to hear them announce the forecast, but will simply take an umbrella anyway.

And returning to the example with the coffee, the person's inquiry as to the milk's freshness is irrelevant if the decision was already made to drink black coffee.

The **sure-thing principle** is one of the most rational ideas in decision theory. It seems logical, and attempts to disprove it seem ridiculous.

Eldar Shafir and colleagues discussed the impact of information in decision making. Here are some examples:

> Imagine that you are on the admissions committee of Princeton University. You are reviewing the file of an applicant who plays varsity soccer, has supportive letters of recommendation, and is editor of the school newspaper. The applicant has a combined SAT score of 1250 and a high school average of B. Would you accept the applicant?

57% of respondents said they would accept him. A second group received a similar question with a bit of extra information:

> Imagine that you are on the admissions committee of Princeton University. You are reviewing the file of an applicant who plays varsity soccer, has supportive letters of recommendation, and is editor of the school newspaper. The applicant has a combined SAT score of 1250 but you have two conflicting reports of the applicant's high school average grade. The guidance counselor's report indicates a B average, while the school office reported an A average. The school has notified you that the records are being checked, and that you will be informed within a few days which of the averages is the correct one.
>
> A. Would you accept this student into the program or wait for clarification from the applicant's school before deciding?
>
> B. If you would wait, would you accept the student if it turns out that the student has a B average?

46% of the subjects said that they would accept him in response to both questions A and B. Although the average of the candidate examined in the second scenario (an A or B average) is better than that of the candidate in the first scenario (a B average), a lower percentage supported this student's acceptance.

In another study which is even more impressive in my opinion, hospital nurses were asked the following question:

> Imagine that your 68-year-old relative is in need of a kidney transplant. A test revealed that your kidney is suitable for donation. Would you donate?

44% of the respondents said that they would donate. A second group received a similar question with a small change:

> Imagine that your 68-year-old relative is in need of a kidney transplant. It's unclear whether your kidney is suitable for donation. A test can be performed in order to determine your suitability. Would you agree to be tested?

69% of respondents said that they were willing to get tested. How could it be that if only 44% are willing to donate a kidney, 69% are willing to get tested? Logically speaking, anyone who is not willing to donate a kidney should also not want to get tested. The researchers proceeded to ask the following question:

> If you agree to be tested, would you donate a kidney if it turns out that your kidney is suitable for donation?

93% of respondents said that they would donate. But this number should be 100%, because whoever gets tested seems to be saying, "If I match, I will donate my kidney, because if I do not intend on donating my kidney, then why would I get tested at all?"

If we want someone to do something for us (for example, something small like donating a kidney…), it's better to ask that person whether they are willing to get tested to see if they are suitable rather than to ask them directly if they are willing to do the thing itself.

Information is perceived as more significant when it is obtained after a test than if it was known beforehand. If the person who needs a kidney was not an immediate relative, most people I know, including myself, would prefer not to donate, but would certainly agree to get tested, hoping to be found unsuitable, and the relative would then find another donor.

The final example of the **sure-thing principle** is extracted from the research of Eldar Shafir and Amos Tversky. A group of students were asked the following question:

> Imagine that you have just taken a tough qualifying exam-
> ination. It is the end of the semester. You feel tired and run-
> down, and you find out that you either passed the exam or
> failed the exam and you will have to take it again in a couple
> of months, after Christmas vacation. You now have an op-
> portunity to buy a very attractive 5-day Christmas vacation
> package to Hawaii at an exceptionally low price. The special
> offer expires tomorrow. Would you take the vacation?

70% of those who were told they had passed the exam said they would go on vacation. The reason for vacation—to celebrate the success of the exam and get drunk. 67% of those who were told they had failed the exam said that they would go on the vacation. The reason for va-cation—to be comforted about failing the exam by going on vacation and getting drunk.

A third group was asked the same question, but was told that the exam results would only be available in a week, and as mentioned, the offer is only valid until tomorrow and they must decide now, before finding out if they failed the exam or passed.

63% of subjects responded that they were not able to decide whether to go on vacation before they knew whether or not they had passed the test. But in practice, if they were told they had passed—they would have gone on vacation, and if they had been told they had failed—they would have gone on vacation. In other words, they would have gone either way. If this is so, then why is it so difficult for them to decide? Because they first need to know the reason for the decision. Are they going out to celebrate the success of the test or to console themselves for failing it? When they go get drunk on a vacation in Hawaii, will it be in the name of joy or sorrow? Either way, it is difficult for people to make a decision without knowing the reason for the decision in advance.

Conclusions:

1. From a logical standpoint, (but not necessarily an emotional one,) before going to get tested for something, one should decide in advance what will be done when the results are known. Do not say, "First I will get tested or test it out and only then I will make a decision." It is worth making decisions regarding every possible result of the test right now. After all, the purpose of the test is to use its results to come to a decision. A test means that if the results are X, I will do such and such, and if Y, I will do otherwise. But if my behavior will be identical in either case, why is the test necessary?

2. If you don't want to buy a car from your relative, don't take it to get inspected at a garage in the hopes of finding out that it's defective.

3. Testing means a commitment to act according to the results.

4. Information gains meaning when it is authorized. People require accredited information in order to make a decision.

5. Oftentimes, people seek out accredited information in order to make a decision even if they have already made up their minds and the added information won't change their decision. The information is required solely to justify the reason for making that decision.

2

Bro, You're my Brother, My Brother

If Alice is taller than Barbara, and Barbara is taller than Cindy, then Alice is definitely taller than Cindy. If Adam got the same test score as Ben, and Ben got the same score as Charlie, then Adam and Charlie have the same test score.

Transitivity means that if A is *something* B, and B is *something* C, then A is *something* C.

If Abe is Bob's brother and Bob is Caleb's brother, then Abe is Caleb's brother. But what exists between siblings does not exist between mothers and daughters: If Amanda is Beth's daughter and Beth is Cynthia's daughter, then Amanda is not Cynthia's daughter.

A friend of a friend is usually a friend, but an enemy of an enemy is not necessarily an enemy. There are aspects and relationships in which **transitivity** apply (i.e., height, siblings, friendships), and there are aspects and relationships in which it doesn't (i.e., motherhood, hostility).

The popular hand game "rock, paper, scissors" is intransitive: Scissors are better than paper, paper is better than stone, but stone is better than scissors.

When it comes to decision making, we want **transitivity** to apply, that is, if Decision A is better than Decision B and Decision B is better than Decision C, then Decision A will be better than Decision C.

Someone is asked whether they prefer drinking orange juice or grapefruit juice, and they choose orange juice. Then they are asked whether they prefer drinking grapefruit juice or lemon juice, and they choose grapefruit juice. So, if orange juice is better than grapefruit juice, and grapefruit juice is better than lemon juice, it makes sense that the person would prefer orange juice over lemon juice.

Unfortunately, **transitivity** doesn't exist in the common methods of decision making we employ. The most common of these is the method of choosing between alternatives according to a number of preferred features. For example, if we have to choose between two cars—one is safer, cheaper, and more beautiful, while the other is merely newer— we will choose the first, because it meets three out of four of the criteria according to which we are basing our decision, compared with the second car which only meets one. This is a very common method in decision making. This is how we choose a spouse, a political candidate, laundry detergent, and a place of work.

The problem with this method is that it highly lacks transitivity. Let's illustrate further with this well-known example of choosing a spouse. Jonah is searching for a wife. He would like to find someone who is wise, beautiful, and wealthy. There are three women—Audrey, who is very wise, beautiful, and poor; Becca, who is dumb, very beautiful, and well off; Claire who is smart, unattractive, and a millionaire.

	Wisdom	Beauty	Wealth
Audrey	Very wise	Beautiful	Poor
Becca	Dumb	Very beautiful	Well off
Claire	Wise	Unattractive	Millionaire

Table 13—Candidate data for Jonah's potential spouses

If he had the option, Jonah would get into deep discussions with Audrey and hang out with Becca all on Claire's dime … but he can only choose one woman. Becca beats Audrey in two out of three qualities (beauty and wealth) and Claire beats Becca in two qualities (wisdom and wealth). The expected conclusion is that if Claire is better than Becca, and Becca is better than Audrey, then Claire is also better than Audrey. But what we will find is that Audrey is better than Claire in two qualities (wisdom and beauty), and thus, Jonah will forever live alone.

A further example of lack of transitivity can be seen in another, very common method employed when making complex decisions where more than one goal is involved.

The previous example contained three goals - wisdom, beauty, and wealth - and the decision was made (or wasn't made) based on the candidate that possessed the most of the favored qualities.

The following example has only two goals: IQ and professional experience. The search here is for a candidate to be an accountant at a reputable company. It was decided that the company would hire the candidate with the highest IQ, but with a caveat: If two candidates have similar IQs (within a ten-point difference), the candidate with more relevant industry experience would be chosen.

Candidate	IQ	Work experience
Alex	115	7
Boris	130	0
Carlos	122	3

Table 14—Candidate data for a bookkeeping position

The first candidate to reach the admissions committee was Alex. He had good data: an IQ of 115 and 7 years of experience. He looked like a promising candidate. (Perhaps this is the place to mention that the company's previous accountant had an IQ of 7 and 115 years of experience.)

The second candidate was Boris. Though he had zero experience, his IQ was 130, and thus he was preferred for the position over Alex. The third candidate was Carlos, who had an IQ of 122 and 3 years of experience. Since the difference in IQ between Carlos and Boris was less than 10 points, and since Carlos had more relevant experience, (3 years compared to Boris's 0,) he was chosen to be the company's accountant.

When Alex heard that Carlos got the job, he returned to the committee and asked that they compare him with Carlos. Indeed, Alex seemed like the better fit over Carlos (who seemed more suitable for the job than Boris, who seems more suitable than Alex). Alex's IQ is only lower than Carlos's by 7 points, and he has 4 years of experience over him. When Boris heard that Alex...

Despite how prevalently employed the method described above is when it comes to making decisions, it leads to a never-ending and inconsistent loop. Most people tend to neglect the slight differences and pay attention to the significant ones.

Let's use the example of buying a used car. If the difference in price is small, we consider the vehicle's mileage. If here, too, the difference is slight, we consider how many previous owners there were. If there isn't much difference here either, we move on to our next consideration.

One of the ways we can overcome the transitive obstacles in the examples above is to use the weighted average method. In this method, a score is given to each desired goal, (in the example of the spouse search, each candidate was scored between 0 and 100 for wisdom, beauty, and wealth,) and in addition, a weighting coefficient is added to each of the goals. What follows is a calculation of the average score of each of the candidates, and the one with the higher score is chosen.

However, this method also has its disadvantages. The first is that a very high score given to an unimportant goal might compensate, so to speak, for a low score given to an important goal. If, for example, we are looking for a doctor to treat immigrants from England, and try to compute the weighted average of the doctor's knowledge in medicine with his level of English, we may get an English linguist who knows how to dress wounds instead of an excellent doctor who does not speak a lick of English.

Another big disadvantage that public decision-makers, and also many researchers of decision making, are mostly unaware of is called "preference dependence." The weight given to a particular goal is dependent on the level of the other attribute. Field Marshal Montgomery once said that a stupid and lazy officer is better than a stupid and diligent officer, because the former at least doesn't cause much harm.

If we tried to weigh intellect and diligence of the officers being selected, we wouldn't have been able to do so since the weight of diligence depends on intellect. If the officer was smart, we would prefer that they be diligent, and if the officer was stupid, we would prefer that they be lazy.

Conclusions:

1. When deciding between different candidates, (a spouse, political candidate, car, workplace, laundry detergent, new basketball player,) and there are several goals to choose from, (for example, in a politician's case—experience, credibility, political position, honesty, leadership,) we need to be sure that the path we choose to making our decision makes sense and fulfills transitivity.

2. Just like every decision-making method containing a multitude of goals, the ever-so-famous weighted average method has its downsides. It's worthwhile to combine different methods. Thus, for example, it is best to activate the weighted average method only once candidates who do not meet the minimum threshold requirements have been rejected.

3

No Smell and No Stench

When you have to choose between two candidates, are you choosing the better one or rejecting the worse one? Is it a positive or negative process?

Optimistic people tend to go with the best option, while pessimists tend to reject the worst. If offered the choice between a $10 cash prize and a one-time coin toss where you could either win $100 or lose $50, (the expected value for tossing the coin is $25,) would you choose the cash or coin toss? An optimistic person would probably compare the potential $100 profit with the safe $10 and go with the coin toss. Someone who is pessimistic will most likely compare the potential $50 loss with the safe $10 gain, and say no to the coin toss.

Amos Tversky, the prominent Israeli psychologist who passed away in 1996, posed the following question, "Which two countries are more similar: West and East Germany, or Nepal and Sri Lanka?"

Most (67%) responded that West and East Germany are more similar. They share a language, culture, legacy, borders, etc. And then Tversky asked, "Which two countries are more dissimilar: West and East Germany, or Nepal and Sri Lanka?"

Here, too, most of the respondents (70%) chose West and East

Germany. One is capitalist and one is communist, one is rich and the other is poor, one is modern and the other is a mess, etc. For different reasons, most of the people claimed that the two Germanies were both more similar to one another *and* more different from one another than the other two countries given in the example.

Based on these results, Eldar Shafir, an Israeli psychologist from Princeton whose research was mentioned in Chapter 1 of this section about the sure-thing principle, conducted an interesting series of experiments on **choosing** and **rejecting**. He asked the study participants the following question:

> Imagine that you are serving in the jury for an only-child sole-custody case following a relatively messy divorce. Parent A has an average income, reasonable rapport with the child, spends little time outside the home, normal working hours, and a good bill of health. Parent B has an above-average income, a very close relationship with the child, spends a lot of time outside of the house, does a lot of work-related travel, and minor health problems.

The participants in the study were split into two groups. The first group was asked to choose a parent they would leave the child with. 64% chose to leave the child with Parent B and 36% chose parent A. The reasons given for choosing Parent B were the above-average income and the closeness of their relationship with the child.

The second group was asked to choose whom among the parents would they take the child away from. 55% chose Parent B while 45% chose Parent A. The reasons provided for rejecting Parent B were absence from home and health issues.

If we combine the percentage of those who would leave the child with Parent B with that of those who would take the child away from

Parent B, we get 119%, compared with merely 81% from combined Parent A answers. If the decisions were made from a rational standpoint, the sum of the numbers should each reach 100%.

	Parent A	Parent B
Income	Average	Above-average
Relationship with child	Good	Excellent
Time outside home	A little	A lot
Work hours	Normal	Busy
Health	Average	Minor problems

Table 15—Data of both parents for a decision regarding custody of their child following divorce

Most people chose Parent B both as the parent that the child should be left with as well as the one the child should be taken away from. Parent A is average, without any prominent features that stand out in or against his or her favor. As my mother would say in Yiddish about some of her acquaintances, "*Er shmakt nicht on shtink nicht*," - "He doesn't smell and he doesn't stink." There are no special reasons for leaving the child in the hands of Parent A, and there are also no special reasons to take the child away from Parent A. On the other hand, there are good reasons for leaving the child in the hands of Parent B, but there are also good reasons to take the child away from Parent B.

If the judge's or jury's decision is determined by **choice**, the child will most likely remain in the hands of Parent B and be taken from Parent A. But if the decision is made through **rejection**, the child will most likely be taken away from Parent B and remain in the custody of Parent A.

A lighter example concerns choosing ice cream: Frozen yogurt tastes good and has little cholesterol, compared with regular ice cream that has an excellent taste but is high in cholesterol. The percentage of people who chose regular ice cream (72%) plus those who rejected it (45%) amounted to 117%, while the percentage of those who chose frozen yogurt (28%) plus those who rejected it (55%) amounted only to 83%.

When doctors make decisions about choosing the proper treatment for a patient, they do so with their eyes set on the future and in hopes of improving the patient's health. Judges, however, when dealing with malpractice suits, consider the doctor's decisions in retrospect, after the damage has already been done. For this reason, courts tend to pay more attention to the potential negative outcomes that come with treatment. In other words, they consider reasons to **reject** treatment. Whereas doctors, who are mainly concerned with the potential benefits, consider reasons for **choosing** treatment, despite the risks involved.

One of the consequences of this gap is that doctors tend to prefer treatments that have higher chances of recovery, and judges tend to search for problems in these treatments because they have higher risk.

Conclusions:

1. We base our decisions on certain reasons. If we are told to choose, we will search for good reasons. If we are told to reject, we will search for bad reasons.

2. A controversial person is more likely to be both chosen and rejected relative to an average person whose chances of being both chosen and rejected are low.

3. Different decisions will be made when we choose between alternatives and when we reject alternatives.

4. When deliberating between two or more alternatives, we should

pose the issue to ourselves as both a choice and as a rejection.

5. It is possible that the manner in which we (as judges) retrospectively examine the behavior of others, may not suit the original deliberation of the decision maker (such as a physician or army commander) at the time that it was made. If the outcome of the decision turns out to be negative, one must be careful not to emphasize only the negative aspects of the decision, but also to examine its positive sides without underestimating them—precisely as it seemed initially to the decision maker at the time the decision was being made. One must be wary not to look at the decision through the eyes of the observer only in hindsight, thus emphasizing the negative aspects of the decision, because things seen from here are not seen from there.

4

Romantic Getaway Weekend at Guantanamo Bay Detention Camp

A man enters a restaurant. "What do you have to eat?" asked the waiter.

"There's beef and chicken," replied the waiter.

"Give me the beef, please," said the man.

After about a minute, the waiter returns and says, "I forgot to mention that we also have an exquisite grilled fish."

"In that case," responded the man, "I'll have the chicken."

What does the fish have to do with deciding between beef and chicken? In fact, one of the basic rationality principles in decision theory holds that the addition of a new option cannot cause an existing option to become more favorable (the **regularity axiom**). For example, a market segment of an existing product will not grow with the introduction of a new product; The ranking of the Israeli song in the Eurovision Song Contest should not improve if a country that has not participated before joins the competition; The addition of an option that no one chose should not affect the choice between existing options.

If I prefer a weekend in Rome over a weekend in Paris, would my preference change if I was also offered a weekend at the Guantanamo

Bay detention camp? Rationally, the addition of the detention camp option should not change my preference between Rome and Paris.

But Amos Tversky and his colleagues, Itamar Simonson (a marketing lecturer at Stanford) and Eldar Shafir, conducted several studies that showed that the regularity axiom is consistently violated."

In one study, students were offered to purchase a popular model of a Sony audio player for a great price of $99. 66% of the respondents said they would buy the device and 34% said they would not.

Another group in the same study were offered a choice between that same popular $99 Sony player and an older Sony model for $95. It would seem that the appearance of the older device shouldn't have had an effect on the desire to purchase the newer Sony, and although nobody chose the old Sony, the percentage of buyers of the new Sony went up from 66% in the first group to 76% in the second group.

The older Sony player acted as a point of reference for the newer model. For merely $4 more, one could purchase a new device instead of an older one. The price seemed reasonable and the new Sony suddenly looked more attractive.

This phenomenon is called the **attraction effect**: The addition of an option which is clearly inferior to an existing option makes the original option more attractive.

Some people were offered the choice to pick between a car that drives wonderfully with a gas mileage of 24 miles per gallon (mpg) and a car that drives well and requires 30 mpg of gas. Half of the respondents chose the first car and half chose the second.

When they added a third vehicle to the pre-existing set of options (decoy 1)—a car that drives wonderfully but has a gas mileage of only 19 mpg—the percentage of people who chose the first car rose from 50% to 70%.

When the researchers added a third vehicle to the pre-existing set of options (decoy 2)—a car that drives terribly and has a gas mileage intake of 30 mpg—the percentage of people who chose the second car rose from 50% to 80%.

	Driving quality	Miles per gallon	% Choice
Car 1	100	10	50% chose Car 1
Car 2	80	13	50% chose Car 2
Temptation 1	100	8	70% chose Car 1 30% chose Car 2
Temptation 2	60	13	20% chose Car 1 80% chose Car 2

Table 16—Example of the attraction effect. Rates of vehicle preferences influenced by the addition of decoys which produce points of reference.

As one can see from Table 16, nobody chose decoys 1 or 2, but their addition led to the choice of a car that seemed relatively superior to them. The decoys serve as points of reference in choosing a vehicle.

Let's assume that a friend of yours is deliberating whether to marry a smart yet poor man or a dumb yet rich man. If you feel that she should marry the smart and poor man, try to introduce her to another bachelor who is not smart and not dumb but is poor. The addition of this third man, who stands out as inferior to the smart and poor man, will make the latter seem more attractive.

In the study involving the Sony player mentioned above, there was also a third group of students. They were offered the option of purchasing the same popular Sony model for $99 or a top-of-the-line Aiwa player for $159. It would seem that, due to the wider variety, the percentage of people who would buy one of the two devices would increase, and that the percentage of those who decided not to purchase either would go down, but what happened? The amount of people who decided not to buy went up from 34% to 46%. This is because, as compared to the first group, the members of the second group had a conflict and a difficult decision in choosing between the popular and cheap Sony and the top-of-the-line and expensive Aiwa. This dilemma led more people to not buy at all. It turns out that as the number of choices increases, so does the tendency not to choose at all or to choose the status quo.

The American psychologist Barry Schwartz even goes so far as to say that even though logic says that if people have more options to choose from, they will be able to choose precisely the options that make them most happy, in actuality, an overabundance of choices can often lead to misery, regret, and even depression. He calls this phenomenon "The Tyranny of Choice."

The researchers Botti and Iyengar title this "The Dark Side of Choice." They claim that when it comes to non-complex problems, it's best to choose among more options, but as the level of complexity rises, having a large number of options can lead to confusion, paralysis in action, or even exhaustion, and the quality of our decision-making drops as a result.

A great example of this is delivered by psychologist Eldar Shafir and Dr. Donald Redelmeier. They asked a group of about 140 doctors the following question:

> The patient is a 67-year-old farmer with chronic right-hip pain. The diagnosis is osteoarthritis. You have tried several nonsteroidal anti-inflammatory agents (e.g., aspirin, naproxen, and ketoprofen) and have stopped them because of either adverse effects or lack of efficacy. You decide to refer him to an orthopedic consultant for consideration for hip replacement surgery. The patient agrees to this plan.

Before sending him away, however, you check the drug formulary and find that there is one nonsteroidal medication that this patient has not tried (ibuprofen).

Do you:

A. Try out the medicine while still sending in the referral for hip replacement surgery?

B. Stick to the original plan and send the referral without prescribing new medicine?

Around half of the doctors (47%) chose Option A, meaning, having the patient try ibuprofen and still sending the referral for surgery, and 53% chose to send in the referral for surgery without testing the medicine.

A separate group of doctors received the same question but with a slight addition. This time, there were two new medications on the menu:

> The patient is a 67-year-old farmer with chronic right-hip pain. The diagnosis is osteoarthritis. You have tried several nonsteroidal anti-inflammatory agents (e.g., aspirin, naproxen, and ketoprofen) and have stopped them because of either adverse effects or lack of efficacy. You decide to refer him to an orthopedic consultant for consideration for hip replacement surgery. The patient agrees to this plan. Before sending him away, however, you check the drug formulary and find that there are two nonsteroidal medications that this patient has not tried (ibuprofen and piroxicam).
>
> Do you:
>
> A. Try prescribing ibuprofen while still sending in the referral for hip replacement surgery?

B. Try prescribing piroxicam while still sending out the referral for hip replacement surgery?

C. Stick to the original plan and send the referral without prescribing new medicine?

Now that the doctors had two medications to choose from, the number of doctors who chose to stick to the original plan and not attempt a new medication rose to 72%.

The lack of ability to decide between two medications led more doctors to stick to the original plan and send the patient to undergo complex surgery, even though simpler options became available.

Ian, an avid soccer fan, is watching a soccer game on TV between Brazil and Argentina on Channel 1. The game is awesome and he is enjoying every moment. Every time his wife requests his attention to discuss their son's low grades in school, Ian reproaches her and claims that he is busy.

Suddenly, the phone rings. It's his good pal Cody, who is also an avid soccer fan. Ian assumes that Cody wants to discuss the game with him and answers the phone. "Hey Ian," says Cody. "Are you watching the game between Germany and Italy on Channel 2?"

Has Ian's situation improved or gotten worse following this telephone conversation?

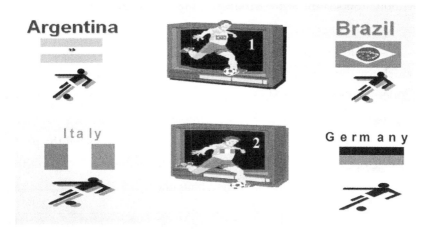

It would seem as though Ian's situation had improved. He can now choose between two quality soccer matches. Logic tells us that the more options we have to choose from, the easier it will be for us to choose the best option for us.

Ian, who is proficient in operating remote controls, switched to Channel 2 for a moment to see what was happening in the game between Germany and Italy. When he switched back to Channel 1, he saw that Brazil had scored a goal and that the score was 1:0. He waited for the replay of the goal, and since it was delayed, he switched back to see what was happening on Channel 2. Italy scored a goal and the score was 1:0.

Ultimately, the game between Argentina and Brazil ended in a tie at 3:3, and the game between Italy and Germany ended with a victory for Italy at 5:2. All in all, 13 goals were made in both games, but he didn't see any of them. He was so upset, that even the conversation about his son's academic future had to be put off for a later date...

Itamar Simonson posed a question in one of his many studies in the field of marketing, asking what people preferred: A) A simple and cheap Minolta camera (X-370) for $170, or B) a medium-quality Minolta (3000i) for $240. Around half of the people chose the cheap camera and about half chose the medium-quality camera.

A separate group was asked to choose between three cameras, two of which were mentioned above and the third was of exceptional quality (7000i) and was being sold for $470.

It would seem, according to the simple rationality principles, that the addition of the expensive camera shouldn't have affected the percentage of those who chose the cheap camera, which was 50% in the first question. In reality, this is what happened:

	Price ($)	% Choice
Minolta (X-370)	170	50%
Minolta (3000i)	240	50%
Minolta (X-370)	170	22%
Minolta (3000i)	240	57%
Minolta (7000i)	470	21%

Table 17—Percentage of buyers of the cheap, medium-quality, and exceptional cameras when the choice is between either two of the cheaper cameras or all three.

The addition of the expensive camera minimized the demand for the cheap camera, but amplified the demand for the medium-quality camera. This phenomenon is called the **compromise effect**. People don't like choosing extreme options. A choice will appear better when it is not extreme. People don't tend to buy the cheapest television ("because it's probably not worth it"), and they don't tend to buy the most expensive one either ("because it's way too expensive"). When sellers want to sell an especially large television, they bring in an even bigger one, not for the purpose of selling it, but only as a reference point.

A similar phenomenon can be seen in the field of law: the story of the murder of a security guard at a certain store was presented before a mock jury. They were asked to determine whether the story of what happened fits the definition of "aggravated murder,"(meaning, a crime attributed to the murder of a police officer, judge, or any law official,) "murder without aggravated circumstances," or just "manslaughter."

A separate group heard the same story, but were asked to determine whether the story fit the definition of "murder without aggravated circumstances," "manslaughter," or "manslaughter under mitigating circumstances."

Table 18 presents the division of responses.

	The severe version	The lenient version
Aggravated murder	13%	---
Murder	57%	38%
Manslaughter	30%	55%
Manslaughter under mitigating circumstances,	---	7%

Table 18—Voter percentage according to how the options are presented

According to simple logic, if "aggravated murder" was not an option, as in the lenient version, the percentage of those who chose "murder" in the lenient version should be more or less the sum of those who chose "aggravated murder" + "murder" in the severe version, meaning, 13% + 57% = 70%.

Lo and behold, the percentage of those who chose "murder" in the lenient version was only 38%. This number was not yielded by the addition of the "manslaughter under mitigating circumstances" option which only received 7%, but by the rise in number for the "manslaughter" option from 30% in the severe version to 55% in the lenient version.

Here, too, one can see that people tend to avoid choosing extreme options. When the option of choosing "aggravated murder" is made available, most people choose "murder," but when the most extreme option is "murder," most people choose the more neutral option, which here is "manslaughter."

The cancellation of an extreme option does not make it such that the next extreme option is chosen, but moves the whole distribution in a more moderate direction.

Conclusions:

1. Oftentimes, an excessive amount of options to choose from leads us to make less calculated decisions.

2. One may decide to limit his options regarding decisions that are not especially important. For example, stick to two stores when shopping for clothes.

3. Learn to be okay with "good enough": Make a choice that suits your primary requirements and do not seek out that elusive "best" choice.

4. Consciously limit your reflections on features that seem appealing for options which you have ruled out. Teach yourself to focus on the positive parts of your choices.

5. Control expectations. The phrase "Don't expect too much and you won't be disappointed" may be a cliché, but it's rational advice for one who desires to live a happier life.

6. As the number of choices increases, so does the tendency not to choose at all or to choose the status quo. If one of your company's most dedicated employees wants to move to another job, make him an alternative offer, and then another. His deliberation between the different options may cause him to stay with you…

7. An overabundance of options also increases the possibility of feeling regret, and often causes frustration.

8. Regarding decisions in which time plays an important factor, such as cancer treatment, it is best to spend a lot of time choosing the doctor with whom you will take the journey and not to ask for additional opinions. The reason for this is if these opinions are different from the opinion of the first doctor, and because doctors envying each other doesn't help the cause, it will only prolong the decision-making process and delay the beginning of treatment.

9. Adding a conspicuously inferior alternative to an existing alternative will make the existing alternative more attractive. In this way, people's choices can be influenced by the addition of alternatives that are significantly inferior to the ones we want.

10. It is worth remembering that we have a natural tendency to not choose extreme alternatives, and to know that we can be fooled by added imaginary alternatives that are used solely to skew our decision.

PART V

PERCEPTION OF RESULTS

1

The Zero Illusion

A few years ago, I was asked to lecture at one of the colleges in exchange for a very high salary. I gladly accepted the offer and after much preparation, arrived to the campus on the first day of the semester. Upon entering the campus I noticed that parking cost $3. The irritable guard at the gate was uninterested as to whether I was a lecturer or a guest. "Whoever doesn't have a sticker has to pay."

What, am I the campus idiot? I thought to myself. I had forgotten that I was about to receive a nice chunk of money for my work in the next few hours, and I began searching for a parking spot outside campus.

In the first lap around campus, I found a parking spot 650 feet away, but I didn't park there in the hopes of finding a closer spot. I didn't, however, find such a spot and expecting the first spot to still be available, I did another loop around campus only to find that the spot had already been taken.

After three more rounds of searching, I ended up parking 1,300 feet away, and I had to race to class, reaching the students sweaty and upset.

Aside from being stingy about my parking ticket, there was something else going on here—a phenomenon called **the zero illusion**. This is a relatively negative feeling that is caused by a minor loss. People don't like losing, even if only on a minor scale.

In the course I teach on decision theory, I open with the following question.

Which would you prefer:

1. To take part in a lottery with equal chances of earning either $100 or $300?

2. To take part in a lottery with equal chances of either earning $1000 or losing $200?

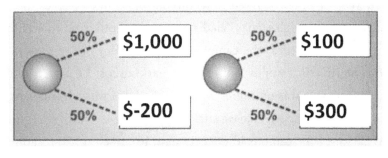

Lottery B   **Lottery A**

The expected profit of the second lottery ($400) is bigger than that of the first ($200), but most of the respondents preferred the lottery with no losses over the one that had a larger expected profit but also a chance of experiencing a minor loss.

During one of my lectures in a very large governmental organization, the CEO of the company attending the lecture shared that he runs two factories: a large one which earns between $2-3 million dollars a year, and a second, smaller factory whose earnings fluctuate between a minor loss ($200,000 a year) and a minor gain ($500,000 a year).

While monitoring his managerial investment in both factories, he discovered that he devoted most of his energy to the smaller factory. Even though the first factory was more profitable and had a potentially greater contribution, it was more important to the CEO to avoid the loss from the small factory than to expand the profit of the larger one.

This can be seen in the following illustration:

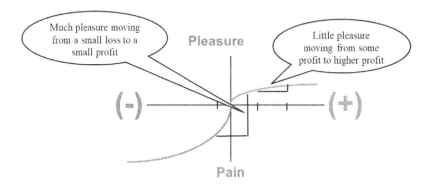

Figure 12—The zero illusion

The pleasure gained in transition from a small loss (-$200K) to a small profit ($500K) is much larger than the pleasure gained in transition from a medium profit ($2M) to a great profit ($3M).

The zero illusion comes into play due to the very steep decline of the line on the left side of zero in the graph.

Due to the fear of experiencing minor losses, people often avoid getting involved in business that has a potential for great profit. A loss—even a small one—stings worse, or at least that's how they think or feel, compared with the pleasure felt from earning a profit that is by far larger.

Dan Ariely and his colleagues offered students to purchase a single type of chocolate. The choice was between a piece of simple chocolate that wasn't particularly tasty for the price of 1¢ and a delicious truffle for 15¢. Most of the students (73%) purchased the expensive chocolate.

A different group of students were offered the choice between the same two chocolates, but this time, the less tasty chocolate was being offered for free and the tasty chocolate for 14¢. Most of the students (69%) preferred to accept the much less tasty but free chocolate.

Conclusions:

1. It is not worth getting worked up over small losses.

2. Fearing a loss can often lead people to avoid very profitable choices because of some minor risk involved.

3. We often invest a lot of time avoiding losses instead of producing profits.

4. The fear of losing $1,000 is often greater than the fear of going from a loss of $10,000 to $11,000.

5. It is not worth getting carried away with enticing offers that seem to be free. Free offers can often lead us to make decisions that don't cater to our original needs.

2

We Regret What We Do in the Short Run and What We Don't Do in the Long Run

Annie never picks up hitchhikers. It was raining heavily one night and a soldier was standing at a junction. He lifted his hand to ask for a ride. Annie stopped for him, and the soldier imposter robbed her of all her money and left.

Beth always takes hitchhikers. It was raining heavily one night and a soldier was standing at a junction. He lifted his hand to ask for a ride. Beth stopped for him, and the soldier imposter robbed her of all her money and left.

Who among the two of them has more remorse over picking up the soldier?

Most people (88%) respond that Annie regrets more. The more active and non-routine the decision, the more remorse is felt.

Regret and disappointment are two negative emotions that derive from the difference between the results of our decisions and the results of what could have happened or of what we expected to happen.

Regret is an emotion that comes with the feeling of "had I acted differently in the past, my situation today or in the future would be better." "I should have done it this way and not the other way." "It's too bad I didn't take an umbrella." "I wish I ordered the schnitzel and not the steak at the restaurant." "I should never have studied medicine."

After love, regret is the emotion that occupies our minds on a daily basis more than others.

Self-blame is the central factor in telling apart **regret** from **disappointment**. If the negative outcome was a result of a decision that was in my control, I would feel remorse. If the negative outcome was not up to me, I would be disappointed.

A man filled out a lottery ticket in which he had to guess the correct results of 16 soccer games, and it turned out that he had been right about 15 games. Suppose that if he had marked that last game correctly, he would have won $3 million—then he would regret the fact that he hadn't marked the last correct response, which in retrospect always seems more obvious.

If someone had guessed all 16 games correctly, he would expect to win a large sum. If, in that same week, a lot of people had succeeded in guessing all of the games correctly, instead of having won $3 million, as was expected, each would only win $33.18. What they would feel then would be **disappointment**. There's nothing to regret. There is nothing that person could have done better.

And the higher the expectation, the greater the disappointment in the event of a failure. A fan of the Italian national football team, who are world champions, would be more disappointed with the team's failure to qualify for the final stage than would a fan of the Turkish team, who lost at a similar stage. The expectations of the Turkish fan were lower and therefore, the disappointment was also lower.

A popular way to avoid disappointment is to not do anything. One who does nothing cannot be disappointed. On the other hand, one who does nothing is prone to regret. Disappointment is measured relative to the expectations of each individual, while regret is measured relative to other choices - the decisions of others, for example.

Lotteries in most countries are based on guessing 6 out of 40 numbers. Suppose that the numbers I chose were 3, 7, 12, 22, 28, 31, and the winning numbers were 2, 17, 20, 32, 39, 41—I wouldn't feel remorse. I wouldn't say to myself, oh no, too bad I chose 3, 7, 12, 22, 28, 31 and not 2, 17, 20, 32, 39, 41. Maybe I feel disappointed, but it's a light disappointment, because I didn't think that the chances of me winning were high anyway.

This is a good place to quote a song written by Yaron London and Nissim Aloni about luck and education:

> In school they teach us not to rely on luck.
> "By the sweat of your brow you will eat your bread."
> Words of wisdom, words well spoken, but what's the problem?
> Of students, there are many, thank heavens,
> Of schools, there are few in session.
> Why? There's no budget.
> What's to be done? A state lottery.
> What for?
> To build schools of which there are not many.
> Why build schools?
> In order to learn and to teach.
> Teach what? To teach not to rely on luck,
> "By the sweat of your brow you will eat your bread."
> Everybody is smart, everybody's waiting on miracles,
> Friday comes along and the heart is in pieces
> And they keep on trying.

The Dutch lottery is a great example of using regret as a means to sell. The first official lotto in the world started in Holland in 1726. There weren't just six random numbers in the lottery, but zip codes. Anyone who lived in the area that was chosen and who had bought a ticket would win a big prize. This lottery is built on the foundations of regret. People fear that they will experience great regret if they don't buy a ticket and their area is chosen in the lottery. And not only do they not win, but they know all the winners because they live in the same neighborhood which may amplify the regret and anger.

Charles and Dan were supposed to fly on two different flights at 8 in the morning. They shared a cab, but due to traffic they arrived at the airport only at 8:30. Charles was told that his flight departed on time, and Dan was told that his flight was delayed and departed at 8:29. Which one of them would be more aggravated? Almost all of those asked (96%) said that Dan would be more aggravated.

The easier it is to imagine a positive outcome and to compare between what happened and what could have happened, the stronger the disappointment and regret. Dan had an easier time imagining a situation in which he was not late to the flight, and therefore an easier time regretting that he left too late to reach the airport. Charles, on the other hand, feels that even if he had left 20 minutes earlier, he still wouldn't have made it on time.

When does a fan of the Chicago Bulls suffer more—after a 20-point loss in a game where the opposing team was leading the whole game, or after a one-point loss in a game where the Bulls were leading and then at the last second, the opposing team scored the winning basket?

In the second example, it is easier to imagine a scenario in which the Bulls won, and therefore it hurts more. The more tangible the loss, the greater the disappointment. But the opposite is also true: The more tangible the possibility of losing, the more luck you feel you have. This is an elevated feeling after experiencing a victory at the last second.

Eddie and Frank were eliminated from the semi-finals of a tennis tournament, both after a tiebreaker. Eddie lost when his opponent hit an ace (a serve Eddie couldn't return), and Frank lost because of a careless mistake that he made. Which one of them will spend more time that night thinking about the game?

Most of the respondents (85%) said that Frank will give himself a harder time. This is because the more active a decision, the more remorse it produces, and the more passive a decision, the less remorse it produces.

Similar results were found by Orit Tykocinski and Noa Steinberg in a study they conducted with students from Ben-Gurion University. A person late to an important flight or meeting due to heavy traffic will feel better than someone who was late because they were held back by a police officer who pulled them over for speaking on the phone while driving. Regret is a heavier negative emotion than disappointment, because it stems from an act that was in our control, while disappointment stems from something that was out of our control.

A study conducted by Ilana Ritov and Jonathan Baron showed that people were reluctant to vaccinate their children against influenza because of a 5 in 10,000 chance that the vaccine would kill the child. But without the vaccine, there was a 10 in 10,000 chance that the child would die from the disease. The probability of the child dying as a result of the vaccine was lower than the probability that the child would die without the vaccine, but remorse over death that was the result of the vaccine was greater than remorse over death that was caused by the disease. In the first case, the parents would blame themselves as responsible for the child's death, and in the second place, the disease would be at fault. They called this phenomenon **omission bias**.

Regret, but also pleasure, stemming from the decision about change, are stronger than regret and pleasure that stem from decisions that don't change the situation. A student that marked the correct answer in a test and then erased it and marked a different answer, feels worse than someone who marked the wrong answer to begin with.

Orit Tykocinski and her colleagues analyzed the subject of regret in the other direction as well. The original perception of regret was that, "If I make a wrong decision right now, I'm likely to regret it in the future." **Inaction inertia**, which these researchers describe, states that if someone misses out on an opportunity and is given another, less favorable one in the same context, that person may not take advantage of the second opportunity, even if it is a positive one, just to avoid feeling remorse.

Someone who missed out on an opportunity to buy a piece of clothing for 50% off, will most likely not buy that same garment for 10% off. Someone who was offered a ticket to a basketball game in the Europe Cup for $30 instead of $100, and forgot to utilize the offer, will most likely not accept a ticket for $70 instead of $100.

The last examples depict **regret in hindsight**. If I purchase the piece of clothing for only 10% off, I will regret now the fact that I didn't buy the garment for 50% off earlier. Someone who buys the basketball game ticket at a price of $70 will feel a $40 weight of regret for not buying the ticket for $30, and will therefore apparently refrain from making the purchase despite the fact that it's still cheaper than a full-price ticket, all in order to avoid a feeling of regret.

Research conducted by Schwartz and colleagues brought to light a significant connection between regret and bouts of depression and neuroses, as well as a reciprocal connection between regret and happiness, optimism and satisfaction from life. Perfectionists are people who also regret a lot. They're more concerned with achieving something great than enjoying something that's very good.

As mentioned, regret is found to be more characteristic of active decisions rather than passive decisions. But studies conducted by Gilovich and Medvec show that this phenomenon is reversed when dealing with a long time frame. In other words: In the short run, people regret things that they did, but in the long run, they regret things that they didn't do. When you ask adults what they regret, they primarily note things they didn't do, such as not having studied study, not getting divorced, or staying at the same job instead of opening their own business. When you ask people what they regret from the past month, they generally regret things that they did, such as leaving their job, hurting someone, or damage they caused.

Conclusions:

1. People tend to refrain from making changes. It's easier for them to be passive and deal with the disappointment, rather than be active and deal with the regret. The more active the decision, the greater the regret.

2. Whoever doesn't make decisions will not be disappointed, but is likely to regret. Therefore, it's best to try and get disappointed then to not try and regret, because it's easier for people to live with disappointment then with regret. Regret is a heavier negative emotion than disappointment. It comes with internal attribution and self-blame in the event of a failure, while disappointment is attributed to an external factor.

3. The greater the probability of success, the greater the disappointment.

4. If we miss out on an excellent opportunity, it doesn't mean that we will miss out on a good opportunity later on. We should neutralize the missed opportunity and consider the new opportunity to be

the first, and not compare it to the former one.

5. A student that received a grade of 95 on an important test can either think about the one question he got wrong and feel regret, or he can enjoy the high grade. Perfectionism is striving to achieve excellent results instead of enjoying very good ones.

6. In the short run, we will regret things that we did, but it's worth remembering that in the long run, we will regret things we didn't do more. Therefore, it's probably best to do them.

7. Disappointment is a sign of there having been high expectations. Even though it's a negative emotion, it is also an expression of having had more ambition and drive to achieve. A life that is full of disappointment is also full of expectations and also full of achievements.

3

Reference Point

Remember the story in the introduction of this book about my vacation in Ko Phi Phi? That moment when the incredible vacation had come to an end, and I discovered that another Israeli couple paid $40 for a room that we paid $60 for? As mentioned, I was mad at my wife during all of dinner for not finding a cheaper room. All the many years of love between us were forgotten, and the painful $20 loss was infuriating to me.

This is a classic example of the effect that reference points have on our emotional state. Meeting this Israeli couple did not change our situation in any way. Nothing bad happened. The owner of the hotel didn't charge us extra, we didn't find any cockroaches in the room, the sheets were clean, the bath had hot water, and everything was exactly the way we had wanted it to be. The only thing that had changed was our point of reference: We suddenly felt as though we had paid too much. We had a basis to compare to, and it made us feel like suckers.

It isn't easy for me to admit, but the opposite situation also happened to me, where people paid more than I on something identical to what I bought, and even though my situation didn't get any better, I was very happy to learn that they paid more than I had to.

Such a tale occurred in Sri Lanka. I traveled there in August of 1988 with my colleague, Eldad, to give some lectures to members of the local Ministry of Agriculture. A day before I returned to Israel, we spent time in the holy city of Kandy. I saw a wonderful leather bag at the Central Market, and I bought it for my daughter for 300 rupees, which was equivalent to around $10 at the time. Eldad liked the bag too and wanted to buy one, but the shop owner didn't have any more, and suggested that we purchase one tomorrow when we reach the capital city of Colombo.

The next day was scorching hot. We left the air-conditioned hotel and stepped into the oven that was the central market. Eldad walked through the alleyways of the market, and I trailed after him, sweaty and out of breath. He found the bag at one of the stands.

"How much?" he asked the merchant.

"360 rupees," answered the merchant.

"My friend bought one yesterday in Kandy for only 300 rupees," Eldad told him.

"So go to Kandy!" the merchant replied.

Eldad tried to bargain with the merchant for a very long time, but the merchant wouldn't budge. The amount I paid for a cold beverage while waiting for him to finish arguing with the merchant was more than the 60 rupees he was trying haggling over so passionately.

As our flight time began approaching, I rushed Eldad to finish, telling him that I was willing to pay the difference and that we just have to get a move on. "It's not about the money," he answered. "It's about the principle."

After his failed bargaining attempt, Eldad ended up paying the 360 rupees, which came out to around $12, and we ran to the hotel.

An hour later, while sitting in the air-conditioned waiting room at the airport, after we received our boarding passes and after we passed through security, I wickedly asked Eldad: "Say, how much did you end up paying for the bag?"

"Oh, he really took care of me, that villain of a merchant. I paid him $12, which is 20% more than what you paid in Kandy."

"You know what?" I told him, "I am willing to buy that bag from you for $25. Are you selling it?"

"Are you crazy?" he said. "A bag like this costs $100 in Israel!"

"Oh really? And how much did it go for in Israel an hour ago when we were at the market?"

"An hour ago, the price for it in Israel was not relevant. Now, as we are about to board a flight to Israel, it is relevant."

During the entire time that we were standing in the Sri Lankan market, Eldad's **reference point** was the price that I had paid for the leather bag. But as soon as the scent of Israel began to sneak up his nose, the point of reference shifted to its Israeli price.

This phenomenon is familiar to many people who return from abroad and regret not buying more gifts for themselves and others. While they were away, they made comparisons relative to the price and availability of where they were, but after returning to Israel, their comparisons shifted to the prices at home.

Christopher Hsee of the University of Chicago asked his students how much they would be willing to pay for a set of dishes with 8 large plates, 8 salad plates, and 8 dessert plates at a home clearance sale. The average price was $33 for the entire set.

Another group was asked how much they would be willing to pay for a set that includes 8 large plates, 8 salad plates, 8 dessert plates, 8 cups—2 of which are cracked, and 8 bowls—7 of which are broken. Despite the fact that the second set includes more items—6 whole cups and one more bowl—the price they were willing to pay for it was only $23.

The reference point of the second set was the complete set, without any cracked and broken items, and this reference point caused the price drop for the second set with the defective items.

In the same study, Hsee showed that people enjoyed an expensive scarf (which costs $45 in the $5–$50 price range) over a cheap coat (which costs $55 in the $50–$500 price range). When people receive gifts, they value them in comparison to other items of the same sort.

People were also willing to pay $2.26 for a small amount of ice cream (200g = 7oz) in a small cup (150g = 5oz) instead of $1.66 for a larger amount of ice cream (250g = 8 oz) in a large cup (300 g = 10 oz). It looks like there's more ice cream in the small cup because it's filled to the brim and spilling over while the large cup isn't even filled up to the end.

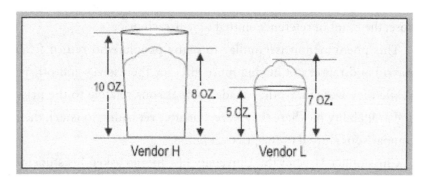

Figure 13—Less is more

In his famous book *Mindless Eating*, Wansink says that based on his research, those who want to lose weight should eat on small plates. This way, the portions will look bigger, and will also be more satisfying.

The most successful example of a reference point, in my opinion, is the feeling medalists experience in the Olympics. As they stand on the podium, we see that the gold (first place) and bronze (third place) medal winners are happy and content, while the silver medal winner (second place) looks depressed and relatively sad. In a study conducted by Madbach and his colleagues, they found that bronze medal winners are happier than silver medal winners.

Silver medal winners compare themselves with gold medal winners and feel as though they missed out, "If only I had tried a little harder," they may say to themselves, "maybe I would have won the gold." Bronze medalists, on the other hand, compare themselves with athletes who came in fourth and won nothing. "What luck," they may think to themselves, "I could have won nothing."

I will end this chapter with an experiment conducted by Dan Arieli and his colleagues. Marketing students studying at Berkeley in California were split into two groups. One group was asked if they would be willing to pay $2 to hear their professor read Walt Whitman poems to them, and the other group was asked if they were willing to come and earn $2 to hear their professor read the poems to them.

3% agreed to pay the amount to hear their marketing lecturer read poetry. It was expected to be a boring event on many levels, but they were willing to pay for it. In contrast, 59% of students surveyed said they would come to hear the professor recite Whitman poems if they were paid $2.

After answering the first question, the same group of students were asked if they would like to come to the poetry reading if it did not involve a fee. Of the students who were initially asked if they would agree to pay for the reading, 35% said they would come. Compare that to the students who were initially asked if they would come to the poetry reading and get paid, of which 8% said they would come.

	Are you willing to pay $2 to hear poetry?	Are you willing to receive $2 to hear poetry?
1) With payment	3%	59%
2) Without payment	35%	8%

Table 19—Example of the effect of reference points on decision-making

The second question was actually identical for both groups. Both were asked if they would come to the poetry reading without payment. The difference between the groups was the point of reference: The first group went from having to pay for the poetry reading to receiving an invitation to a free show; the second group went from being paid to hear the poetry read to showing up for free.

Those who had agreed to pay $2 were happy to come and hear their lecturer read poetry excerpts for free (35%), but very few of those who agreed to receive $2 were willing to hear their lecturer read poetry excerpts for free (only 8%).

The reference point is probably the most influential factor in the way we experience joy or sadness. The decision-making process is always done in comparison to some reference point. When we move apartments, we compare the new apartment to the old one and feel happy. After a while, as we begin to acclimate to our new home, we start comparing our apartment to that of our neighbors, and, as we know, the grass is always greener over there.

Even while driving on a busy road, we enjoy the fact that our lane is advancing quicker than the one next to us more so than we enjoy the fact that traffic is moving quickly at all. The point of reference is not the speed at which we drove home from work yesterday, but the speed that the car next to us is driving at today.

Conclusions:

1. There is an ancient Persian saying about a man who was depressed over the fact that he didn't have any shoes to wear until he met a man who had no legs. We define things as being 'good' or 'bad' subjectively, relative to other things, and not objectively, relative to its "true" value.

2. *Don't judge a book by its cover.* It isn't just the book's cover that influences our decisions, but also the relationship between the cover and what's inside the book: A normal amount of ice cream in a large cup will come across as a smaller amount than normal. In the field of marketing, a large package for a small amount of product creates a reference point that comes with expectations which if not fulfilled, will lead to disappointment. In order to enjoy life, it's best to do less comparisons.

3. When you are abroad (in countries where the prices are cheaper than in the country you came from), buy more presents. When you get back home, you won't regret it. In fact, the opposite will occur—comparing the prices will only make you happy.

4

Why is Wine Sipped and Bitter Medicine Gulped?

Which would feel better—getting a raise from $1,000 to $2,000 or a raise from $4,000 to $5,000? Most people would say that the additional $1,000 is more significant when the salary is low than when it is high. This is not only due to the difference in rates of the raise—100% in the first case and only 25% in the second. The main reason is that we buy all of the more important things with our base salary—like food, clothing, and education, and with any leftover money, we buy less important things such as entertainment and jewelry.

It can be said that the marginal pleasure we feel from making money diminishes. Sure, we will always be happy to accept more money, but the pleasure obtained from each additional dollar declines as money piles up. This works the same way for positive things in life: The pleasure from having an extra week to stay in Europe for vacation diminishes the longer the trip is extended. If someone won a free trip to Europe for a week, they would be really happy to learn that the prize grew to two weeks. On the other hand, if someone won a three-week trip, they would be less happy to learn that their trip was suddenly extended to four weeks.

The phenomenon of **marginal utility** exists also in a negative way: Aaron was sentenced to one year in prison for injuring a pedestrian while drunk driving. He appealed in civil court and his sentence was extended to two years of active jail time. Billy was given a 3-year sentence for killing a pedestrian while drunk driving. He appealed in civil court, and his sentence was extended to four years of active jail time.

Which of them feels worse? Most people would say that Aaron's situation is more difficult. Even though both of their sentences were extended by a year, the transition from one to two years is harder than the transition from three to four years.

This behavior is observable in Figure 14 using the value function of prospect theory developed by Daniel Kahneman and Amos Tversky.

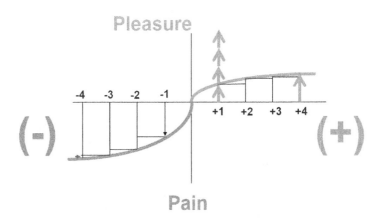

Kahneman and Tversky, 1979

Figure 14—Value function of prospect theory

As can be seen from the right side of the function, marginal pleasure decreases, as does marginal pain on the left side of the function. We can see moderation on both sides of the graph. Here are some examples from the left side: Anybody would admit that the hard part about growing bald is the beginning—the shiny circle that forms at the center of the scalp resembling the forehead of a Jesuit Monk. It's unpleasant when it continues growing, but the level of pain diminishes until we grow accustomed to the baldness. The same can be said about wrinkles, gray hair, financial losses, and even casualties of war. The names of the first Americans killed in Iraq were emphasized in the press. With time and with the rising death toll, pain felt for those who perished in war began to decline.

Similar to the **zero illusion**, financial loss hurts a lot when it's minor. As it gets bigger, at the stock exchange for example, pain from additional losses becomes more moderate.

A phenomenon that stands out in the field is called the **sunk cost fallacy**: the tendency to continue with a task after already investing time and energy in it. This phenomenon is also often called the **Concorde effect** named after the airplane that cost a fortune, and thus, due to a commitment to the initial investment, they continued building and even flying it, until it was grounded.

In 1969, Henry Kissinger, the United States foreign minister, said about President Richard Nixon, with reference to the Vietnam War, "He could not just pull out the American troops and betray all 30,000 men who had already died in the cause," and that they had to remain there until victory was achieved. By the end of the war, the number of American casualties hit 58,226, and another 300,000 were injured, and we must not forget the 4 million Vietnamese people who were killed during the war and the millions injured.

A few years ago, one of the women who worked at the same college as me came in sporting a new, bright red hair color. I asked her, "Tell me, Tali, do you really like that color?"

"I hate it!" she answered immediately.

"So why don't you dye it again?"

"Do you know how much this cost me?"

Tali explained that dying her hair had cost $210. If she were to wear her hair in this color for one day, that one day would cost her $210. If she waited two days, it would cost her $105 per day, and if she waited a week, it would cost her only $30 per day. After a light calculation, she came to the conclusion that even though she would suffer for two weeks, it would bring the price down to $15 a day which seemed like a fair price...

Allan Teger was a professor of psychology at the University of Pennsylvania. (Today, by the way, he takes artistic photos in the nude, which teaches us that there is life after academia.) In 1980, he published a book called *Too Much Invested to Quit*. The book, for the most part, was about the dollar auction—a public auction for a one-dollar bill. The rules are as follows: Whoever offers the highest price for the one dollar, receives the dollar and pays the price that he offered for it. The person who offered up the second-highest price also pays the price they offered, but doesn't win anything. The auction begins and somebody bids 10¢. Another one bids 60¢, and someone else 90¢. The one who bid 60¢ can quit and lose 60¢ or can raise to $1 and leave even. This person of course prefers to bid the dollar for the dollar and not lose his 60¢. The person who bid 90¢ can quit and lose that sum of money or can bid $1.10 in exchange for the dollar, and then they would only lose 10¢, and that's what they do. If the public auction were to finish at this point, the person who bid a dollar would lose it, and that's why it's worth raising the bet to $1.20. And this is how the public auction continues for this one dollar.

When I was studying to earn a Doctorate of Business Administration at the Harvard Business School, my professor for decision theory was Howard Raiffa, who wrote the first books in the field and was a one-of-a-kind lecturer. He played the dollar auction with us and had to stop when the price reached $5.30 against $5.20. To remind you, this was an auction for purchasing one single dollar. Whoever had the bid of $5.20 intended to raise to $5.40 because if they would win, their loss would be $4.40 instead of $5.20.

This was a light example of **crisis escalation**. Zeev Maoz, a scholar of political science, uses this paradox to describe situations in which we are standing opposite an enemy, and both sides prefer to avoid threats, each one wanting the other to back off. In many cases, it all ends in a fight which both sides would've liked to avoid, but couldn't.

And this is how we tend to act when it comes to lost investments:

1. Past investments and efforts seem pointless if we quit without having achieved anything.

2. We continue investing in deals which we know are unwise to pursue, in the hopes that we will succeed to justify or return investments from the past.

3. The bigger our investment in the past in a certain area, the bigger the feeling of obligation to continue investing in this area.

4. We often say, "We've already invested so much..." whether consciously or not, in order to force ourselves to continue when times are rough.

5. It's especially hard for us to quit cold turkey without trying one more time. It's hard for us to accept the fact that we failed, and even harder for us to accept the fact that we shouldn't have done it to begin with.

I conducted a study with my friend Ada Lampert from the Ruppin Academic Center about the connection between parental investment and risk-taking regarding their family's lives. We found that women, due to their deeper investment in birthing and raising children compared with men, would take more risks upon themselves in order to protect their investment. For example, we asked the following question:

> Suppose that your child has a kidney disease which could lead to requiring dialysis twice a week for her whole life. A specialist doctor said that if you donate one of your kidneys to your child, there's an 80% chance that she would make a full recovery and a 20% chance that the child's situation wouldn't change.
>
> The doctor also said that there's a 50% chance that the child would overcome the illness even without an implant, which would be known within two years. If we find out that the child did not get better within two years, we could still do the implant but the chances of success drops to 60%. What would you decide?
>
> 1. I would donate my kidney right now.
> 2. I would wait two years and then donate my kidney if there is a need.
> 3. I would not donate my kidney and hope that the child gets better on their own.

Most of the women (68%) chose to donate their kidney, and the rest (32%) chose to wait two years. Most of the men (56%) chose to donate their kidney, some (41%) chose to wait two years, while the rest (3%) chose not to donate at all. It should be noted that the statistical difference between men and women was significant.

And going from life investments to investments in the stock market—after a big drop in the stock exchange, investors avoid selling their shares. Research shows that those who need the money and have to sell, will sell a share that earned and not one that lost. This phenomenon costs investors a lot of money in avoided profits. As soon as an initial loss hits, any following losses seem smaller. The rise of a stock returning to its former value seems larger than the fall of a stock that continues plummeting in value. When pain reaches a peak, additional losses or other negative results won't exacerbate the pain. This is the point where **there is nothing to lose**.

A not-too-painful example of this is of a soccer match in which the opponent is leading 1:0 and the game is in minute 80 out of 90. Usually in cases like this, the weaker team's coach switches out the defensive players for offensive players, neglecting the defense, sending the whole team into attack mode, and taking chances they didn't take earlier. What's the worst that could happen at this point—that the other team will score another goal and win with 2:0 instead of 1:0? There's no difference. There's nothing left to lose this close to the end of the game.

When an enemy or business rival feels that they are in a situation where they have nothing to lose, like Samson among the Philistines, they may behave in a way that will bring disaster upon themselves and their environment. If a lifer has no hope of ever being released, he may harm other inmates and wardens. What does he have to lose? Would he fear two life sentences?

> Two inmates were sentenced to lengthy prison terms for multiple robberies they committed. The first was sentenced to 29 years in prison and the second to 30 years. The second said to the first, "Take the bed by the door, you're out first."

On the plus side, the diminishing marginal pleasure raises additional implications in decision making. The most important one is the aversion to risk in the positive domain—in other words, when experiencing pleasure.

Suppose you won a two-week trip to Europe. Would you agree to replace it with a lottery ticket where there are equal chances of winning a month-long vacation and wining nothing at all? The thousands of people whom I asked this question answered negatively. Everybody preferred the definite two-week vacation over the uncertain one-month one. A bird in the hand is worth two in the bush.

Most people would prefer receiving $1000 in cash over a lottery ticket where one could win $2000 or nothing at equal chances. As can be seen from the value function, the transition from 0 to $1000 is steeper than the transition from $1000 to $2000.

We tend to avoid risks in order to achieve a sure profit, which is why we prefer certainty over uncertainty and generally refrain from taking risks in positive situations.

Another idea is **segregation of gains**. Boaz Keysar of the University of Chicago, Daniel Gilbert, author of the famous book *Stumbling on Happiness*, and others ask the following questions: Is it better to get married on Valentine's Day or to enjoy each event (wedding and holiday) separately? Is it better to go to a concert and also picnic in a park or maybe it's better to attend a concert and go on a picnic separately, a few weeks apart? Is it better to buy a child two scoops of ice cream at a basketball game or buy one scoop of ice cream twice? Is the enjoyment of having twins greater than that of having two babies born in different years?

The responses of most people who are asked the above questions suggest that one and then another one is better than two. Pleasure is maximized when the benefits are segregated.

How does one drink good wine? In small sips. If we drink the whole cup in one go, we will enjoy at the level of the arrow above number 4 in Figure 14 on page 183. On the other hand, if we drink four-fourths of the cup gradually, we would experience a level of enjoyment at the level of the arrow above number 1 four times. Since the slope in the graph plateaus as it travels right, it is better to enjoy a fourth of a cup four times than to enjoy the whole cup all at once.

A few years ago, I was sent by the Ministry of Foreign Affairs to give a series of lectures in Ethiopia and Eritrea. While in Asmara, I stumbled upon a shop of a local jeweler who designed stunning silver jewelry. I bought my wife a matching set of earrings, bracelet, and necklace. When I returned to Israel, I gave her the earrings. A week later, I gave her the bracelet, and only two weeks later did I give her the necklace as well. My wife got excited each time all over again and asked me why I didn't give her all three pieces of jewelry at once. I explained the theory of **segregating gains** and she smiled understandingly.

A year later, the Foreign Ministry sent me again to lecture in Nepal. Just like before, I bought my wife a matching set of earrings, bracelet, and necklace, this time made from turquoise stone. When I returned to Israel and gave her the earrings, she said, "You can give me the whole set. I already know the theory."

The book of Genesis (32:12–21) tells the story of Jacob's arranged meeting with his brother

Esau after he bought the birthright from him in exchange for lentil stew. Jacob fears that Esau will take revenge on him for stealing the birthright and sends gifts to Esau:

> Please deliver me from the hand of my brother, from the hand of Esau, for I fear him, that he may come and attack me, the mothers with the children. But you said, 'I will surely do you good . . . and from what he had with him he took a present for his brother Esau, two hundred female goats and twenty male goats, two hundred ewes and twenty rams, thirty milking camels and their calves, forty cows

and ten bulls, twenty female donkeys, and ten male donkeys. These he handed over to his servants, every drove by itself, and said to his servants, "Pass on ahead of me and put a space between drove and drove." He instructed the first, "When Esau my brother meets you and asks you, 'To whom do you belong? Where are you going? And whose are these ahead of you?' then you shall say, 'They belong to your servant Jacob. They are a present sent to my lord Esau. And moreover, he is behind us.'" He likewise instructed the second and the third and all who followed the drove, "You shall say the same thing to Esau when you find him, and you shall say, 'Moreover, your servant Jacob is behind us.'" For he thought, "I may appease him with the present that goes ahead of me, and afterward I shall see his face. Perhaps he will accept me."

"And put a space between drove and drove." This is the key phrase—don't give Esau all the presents at once but split them up.

If you are going to give someone a gift or bonus or anything else positive, you should split the gift into several components and divide them. It's better to give the waiter a tip of two $20 bills and another $10 instead of one $50 bill.

Richard Thaler, an economist at the University of Chicago, who won the Nobel Prize in Economic Sciences in 2017, posed the following question:

One person was given a lottery ticket and won $75. A second person was given two lottery tickets and won $50 in one and $25 in the other. Which of them is happier?

18% said the former, 64% said the latter, and the rest said there was no difference between the two.

People prefer to enjoy a little for a long time (or many times) than to enjoy a lot for a short time (or once).

Another question:

One man received a letter from the Internal Revenue Service stating that he owed them $100. That same day, he also received a letter from Social Security stating that he owed them $50. A second man was notified by the IRS saying that he owed them $150. Which of them is more upset?

76% said the former, 16% said the latter, and the rest said there was no difference between the two.

People prefer to suffer a lot for a short time (or once) than to suffer a little for a long time (or many times).

This phenomenon of preferring a lot of suffering for a short time over a lighter but lasting suffering is called the **integration of losses**.

How does one drink bitter medicine? In one gulp, unlike good wine. And how does one remove a wax strip from their leg? In one swift motion.

If someone is unfortunately obligated to cause pain to another person, it's best to concentrate the pain and not divide it into portions. If someone has to fire employees or cut salaries, it's best to do it in one shot and not draw out the process. This statement, however, contradicts with Dan Ariely's observation of, "Every day, I had to have a soaking bath that involved removing my bandages and scraping off my dead skin and flesh. The nurses would rip off the dressings all at once, without a break. It was excruciating, but the nurses insisted that tearing the bandages off was the best way."

Why did God inflict ten plagues upon the Egyptians, one after another? Why didn't they make a deal—10 plagues for the price of 8? If God wanted them to suffer less, he would have set them up with a package deal, but since He wanted them to suffer more, He divided up the suffering and thus amplified it.

About a year ago, a student of mine told me that his 18-year-old daughter was sick with cancer and was told that she had to undergo 8 treatments of harsh chemotherapy. When she completed them, the doctor told her that in order to ensure success of the treatments, she would have to go through two more. The girl broke down and showed adamant resistance to continuing treatment, and only after much prying, love, and convincing did she ultimately agree to continue. In the end, she made a full recovery.

I think that the doctor should have told her that he expected that she would need 12 treatments, and after she had undergone 10 treatments, tell her that the final two were extra. 12 - 2 looks a lot better than 8 + 2. This is a type of manipulation, but don't the ends in this case justify the means?

On the negative side of the value function, we can also see the phenomenon of preferring uncertainty over certainty, and the tendency to take risks. People prefer taking risks in order to avoid certain losses.

A group of people were asked two questions:

(1) "Which would you prefer—a certain profit of $240 or a lottery ticket that has a 25% chance of winning $1,000?"
Most people (84%) preferred to take the sure sum of $240.
(2) "Which would you prefer—a certain loss of $750 or a 75% chance of losing $1,000?"

Most people (87%) preferred not to pay the sum of $750 and to take the chance of having to pay $1,000.

A person who is sentenced to one year in prison and has the option to appeal the severity of the sentence with equal chances of being released or serving two years, is likely to appeal.

Another thought related to spending: An expense seems smaller when attached to a big expense. Ofer Azar from Ben-Gurion University showed that people are less troubled by spending a few thousand dollars when they buy a house for hundreds of thousands of dollars than when they buy, say, a used car for only thousands of dollars.

An expense, like a lot of things, is measured relatively and not absolutely. If someone wants his employer to swap his computer screen out for a flatter one, he should ask for a new computer. The cost of upgrading the screen will seem small relative to the price of the computer. For a couple buying a house, they should make sure that the price of having a lawyer to manage the contract of the sale will be included in the price of the house. In general, it's easier to tell the seller to include all kinds of extras in the total price, because if we ask for them after agreeing upon a price, the seller will have a hard time giving them without additional payment.

In 1980, after we left the kibbutz we had been living on, and I was given a vehicle from my place of work, we went searching for a car for my wife. Since we were broke, we arrived at a very used car lot. They showed us two vehicles that suited our budget. One was small with two doors and cost $6,000 and the other one was a little bigger with four doors and cost $7,000. My wife, who wanted the bigger car, said, "You only buy a car once in a while. Let's put in a little extra effort and purchase the more expensive car. We have to take out a loan anyway." I felt as though our budget for the next 10 years was teetering and I asked, "Do you really think it's worth paying $500 for a car door?" I saw a light hesitation on my wife's face, and we ended up buying the smaller car.

The difference between $6,000 and $7,000 seems small. On the other hand, a $1000 expense is perceived as much more, as is the pain felt from spending a lot of money.

The process of making decisions when it comes to negative results is very different than when dealing with positive results. The following table sums up the differences between decisions to be made in the positive realm and those in the negative realm:

Positive	Negative
Marginal pleasure is decreasing	Marginal suffering is decreasing
Earnings seem smaller when attached to big earnings	An expense seems smaller when attached to a big expense
We prefer to divvy up pleasures	We prefer to concentrate suffering
We prefer certainty over uncertainty and tend to avoid taking risks	We prefer uncertainty over certainty and tend to take risks
Pleasure from success is relatively lower then suffering from failure	

Conclusions:

1. If we made a bad decision and lost money, it's the wrong move to continue spending money only because we had already invested in it and are trying to save the investment. We should use the present as a point of reference, and understand that what we already lost—we lost, and that making an additional investment at this time is only worth doing if there is potential to profit right now.

2. We have a tendency to avoid taking risks when it comes to positive results. In order for people to take risks, the expected profit must be significantly higher than the risk-free profit since the suffering of loss outweighs the pleasure of profit.

3. We have a tendency to take risks when it comes to negative results.

4. The more good we experience, the less we enjoy any additional wins, since the marginal pleasure goes down.

5. The more we lose, the less we suffer from any additional losses, because the marginal suffering goes down.

6. Good things should be split up into small portions: Good wine should be drunk slowly, and treats should be given in stages.

7. Bad things should be aggregated using the "Rip the Band-Aid off" method, such as when drinking bitter medicine.

8. An expense will seem smaller when attached to a large expense. But the two expenses should be isolated and regarded separately, and only in this way should decisions be made for each of them.

9. People refrain from selling losing shares, because an additional loss hurts them less than the expected pleasure from the profit returning and balancing them out.

10. If one must sell shares because their forecast is negative, it's worth selling them even if their value has dropped a lot lately; and if one must hold onto a share because it has a positive forecast, it's best to avoid selling even if the value has risen a lot lately.

11. The actual economic value of an expense is absolute and not relative. Spending an extra $300 on better hotels on a trip is exactly the same as spending an extra $300 on purchasing a house.

5

The Bitterness of Failure Outweighs the Sweetness of Success

In the value function presented in the previous chapter (Figure 14 on page 183), an asymmetry can be seen between the right side and the left side, that is, between the positive side and the negative side. The bitterness of failure is greater than the sweetness of success. The pain we feel as a result of a loss is greater than the pleasure caused as a result of a profit of the same weight.

See the demonstration of this in Figure 15:

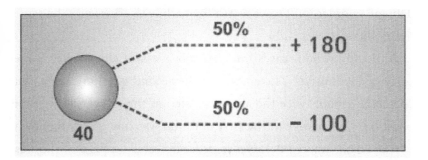

Figure 15—A lottery example

Figure 15 presents a lottery in which there are equal chances of winning $180 or losing $100. Most of the people I asked (including myself most of the time), would prefer not to take part in this lottery, even though the expected profit—the average profit—is positive and equal to $40.

The pain we expect to feel as a result of losing $100 seems greater to us than the pleasure that we would feel as a result of winning $180.

This phenomenon, in which losses appear greater than equivalent gains, is called **loss aversion**. According to this theory, the ratio between the feeling of pain when losing and the feeling of pleasure when winning is 1:2. In other words, the suffering caused by a loss of $100 is equal in intensity as the pleasure caused by a gain of $200.

In one particular experiment, imaginary jurors were asked what amount of compensation someone should get after being injured in a car accident. The study participants acting as the jurors were given a detailed account of the injury and were asked to estimate the amount that would constitute fair compensation for the damage caused to the injured individual. The average amount they offered was about $150,000. Another group of jurors was asked a similar question, but instead of being asked what amount the injured person should be compensated, they were asked what amount they themselves would demand in order for it to be worth their while to experience the same injury themselves.

Although in both cases the question is essentially, "What is the price of the injury?" The answer to the second question was about $330,000—about twice the amount stated in the answer to the first question. The answer to the first question was how much money a person who is injured deserves in order to feel like a person who was not injured. And the answer to the second question was what the cost of the injury is, or how much will a person who has not yet been injured require in order to agree to be injured. The damage caused by the injury before it occurred was perceived as double the damage caused by the injury after it had already occurred.

The relatively low pleasure of positive things and the relatively high pain of negative things also affect negotiation processes. Take, for example, peace talks with an enemy. Everything you give seems large, and anything you get seems small.

Many studies have been done on the differences between the maximum price a person is willing to pay for something and the minimum price a person is willing to pay for giving up the exact same thing. We usually demand more for the sale of an object than we are willing to pay for it. This phenomenon is called the **endowment effect**.

One of the more well-known experiments in this area is the mug study: Students of economics at Cornell University were split up into two groups. One group received a mug with the university symbol on it and the second group didn't receive a mug. Those who received the mug agreed to sell it for an average price of $7, while those that did not receive a mug agreed to pay around $3 for it. If so, what is the true price of the mug—its buying price or its selling price?

Richard Thaler, the one who coined the phrase *the endowment effect*, brings additional examples:

While Mrs. Tony was debating whether to buy a particular device, the seller came and suggested that she buy it, and said that if she was unsatisfied, she could return it within two weeks. The seller knows that Mrs. Tony will get used to the device, and giving it up will be harder than not buying it in the first place.

Mr. Spiegel, an avid wine lover, bought a case of 12 bottles of fine wine in 1970 at a price of $5 per bottle. A few years later, a wine collector offered him to buy each bottle for $100. Mr. Spiegel refused to sell the fine wine, even though he had never bought a bottle of wine for more than $35.

Eldar Shafir and Richard Thaler asked wine collectors how much a bottle of wine bought 25 years ago for $20 was worth today, with a current market price of $75. Some collectors were asked what the value of the bottle would be if they drank the wine or gave it as a gift to a friend, and some were asked what the value of the bottle would be if it fell and broke.

Only about 25% of the first group—those who drank the wine or gave it as a gift—said the value of the bottle was $75. In contrast, 55% of participants from the second group said that the damage caused by the bottle falling and breaking is $75. More than double thought that the value of a broken bottle was worth more than its value if it was consumed or given as a gift.

Mood also has a strong effect on the endowment effect. A study by Zhang and Fishbach found that the endowment effect is especially strong when people are in a negative mood. In the study they conducted, subjects were divided into three groups.

The first group was asked questions which cause a negative mood, such as, "Have you lost someone very close to your heart?" "Do you often feel ignored?"

The second group was asked neutral questions, such as, "How many states are there in the United States?" "Who was the first president of the United States?

The third group was asked joking questions that cause good moods, such as, "What happens if a zebra and a crocodile mate?"

After all the groups answered the questions, the subjects were asked to give a maximum price they would be willing to pay for a quality pen, and a minimum price they would ask for if selling it. Results of the questionnaire appear in Table 20.

	Mood		
	Negative	Regular	Positive
Buying price	$0.85	$1.69	$1.85
Selling price	$3.40	$2.76	$1.58

Table 20—Buying and selling prices of a pen according to mood

Table 20 shows that the difference between the selling and buying price decreases as the mood improves: The buying price is lowest in a negative mood and highest in a positive mood. In contrast, the selling price is extremely high in a negative mood and very low in a positive mood. It turns out that the endowment effect is very strong when the mood is negative, weakens when the mood is neither positive nor negative, and reverses when the mood is positive. When we are in a good mood, we care less about making mistakes, and we are willing to buy more expensively and sell cheaper.

By the way, it turns out that **loss aversion** and the **endowment effect** are not just human traits.

In studies conducted with monkeys involving apple slice selection, it was found that they, too, behave according to the theory—that the loss of an apple slice was experienced as more difficult than the feeling of pleasure in receiving another slice. Similarly, the monkeys who received fruit preferred to eat the slices instead of trading them for grains, but when they were given grains, they preferred to eat the grains and not trade them for fruit.

Conclusions:

1. Groucho Marx followed by Woody Allen said that they would not want to be accepted as members of a club that would agree to accept them. The value of something when it is not in our possession always seems much greater than when it is in our possession.

This is true regarding cars, houses, and love.

2. We are willing to pay a much lower price for something than the price we would charge for its sale. This should make us think about how much this thing is really worth to us.

3. We exaggerate in our assessment of pain caused by losses and failures relative to how we assess pleasure caused by gains and successes. This asymmetry prevents us from taking risks.

4. Even though our emotions tell us otherwise, money that has not entered the pocket has the same value as money that has left the pocket.

5. When negotiating, it is worth remembering that what we give appears to be more expensive than it seems to the recipient, and what we receive appears to be cheaper than it seems to the giver.

6. Whoever we do business with should be in a good mood. He will then be willing to sell cheaper and buy more expensively.

7. Marketing people use the endowment effect when offering the buyer a period in which the purchased product could be returned. This makes the purchase easier since it is perceived to be risk-free, but once the product becomes the buyer's property, it is more difficult giving up the product than it was prior to the purchase.

6

I Hereby Confirm What I Already Know

I came back to Israel 40 years ago after studying in the United States. The banks in the U.S. have an excellent custom: At the end of every month, they send customers all the checks they used. This serves as confirmation of payment for the customer and makes it easier to monitor expenses.

When I returned to Israel, I found that there was only one bank that sends customers their checks. It was called the American-Israeli Bank. I chose to open an account with them for this reason. After a few months, the bank ceased offering this vital service, but I continued being their customer for many years until they merged with a different bank.

A similar thing happened to me with a newspaper subscription, an internet service provider, and a cell phone company. It's relatively easy switching newspapers, but one must get accustomed to the new newspaper format. Changing an internet service provider or cell phone company is already a bit more complicated: Up until recently, you had to change your email address and notify everyone.

Cell phone companies opposed the mobility of telephone numbers, and justifiably so, according to them. They understood that this would weaken the **status quo bias**—the tendency to stay in the same situation we find ourselves in and not to change it.

Those who remain in the same place generally don't upset their environment or enemies. If it's customary in a certain town not to make noise on Sunday afternoons, someone who blasts their radio during those hours should expect to be met with neighborly complaints.

On October 15 in 1962, an American reconnaissance aircraft discovered that nuclear rocket bases were being built in Cuba, only 120 miles outside of the United States. This took place at the height of the Cold War between the Soviet Union and the United States, and raised fears that if America would actively respond, it would lead to World War III. President Kennedy decided, with the help of his consultants, to adopt status quo policies: He did not open fire on Cuba or the Soviet Union by his own initiative, but imposed a naval boycott on Cuba declaring that any ship nearing the border will be inspected, and if weapons were found, they would not be allowed to continue their journey.

Imposing this boycott was a passive deed, one that maintains the existing situation. On the other hand, trying to break the naval boycott would be an active deed which may aggravate the situation.

In a lovely study conducted by researchers from Ben-Gurion University and Hebrew University, the researchers examined the behavior of goalkeepers when facing an 11-meter kick (penalty kick). The findings were intriguing. It was discovered that in most of the cases, the goalie leaps to one of the goal's sides, but had they stayed in place, they would've prevented more goals. The reason for this is because of the goalies' desire to give an impression that they are doing something active towards protecting the goal, and if they were to have stayed in the center, it would appear as though they weren't making enough of an effort.

A class of students from the University of Victoria in Canada were given a choice between receiving a pretty mug bearing their university emblem or a fancy Swiss chocolate bar. A little more than half of the students (56%) chose the mug and the rest chose the chocolate. Students from another class were given the mug as a present. After a few minutes, they were asked whether they would like to replace the mug with the chocolate bar. A whopping amount (89%) chose to keep the mug. Students from a third class were given the chocolate as a present. After a few minutes, they were asked whether they would like to replace the chocolate with the mug. Most of the students (90%) chose to keep the chocolate.

The conclusion is that students simply prefer what they already have. It turns out that switching the item doesn't seem worth it to both those who received the mug and those who received the chocolate.

The **status quo bias** is likely to cause people to become stagnant or freeze up. Here's an example from the military:

> A rumor was going around about an Israeli Artillery Corps commander who was being hosted in England and observing a shooting practice. When the commander yelled, "Fire!" the sergeant raised his hand as if holding something up in the air. When the Israeli guest inquired about the reason for the hand raising, the sergeant looked shocked and asked, "Don't sergeants in Israel raise their hands during fire?" The Israeli commander asked both junior and senior officers about the hand raising but no one knew the reason. That evening, the Israeli guest met with a veteran of the British Artillery Corps who had even served in World War I. When he asked the elderly man to settle the matter, he replied, "If the horses are not restrained, they will jump during fire."

In the previous chapter, we saw that suffering as a result of a loss is greater than pleasure derived from profit, and that the selling price for anything is bigger than its buying price. Someone who replaces an object with another gets to enjoy receiving something new, but suffers from having given up the object they had to begin with. Less pleasure is felt from receiving something than the pain felt from losing something, and therefore, our tendency is to stay in the same place, in other words, to not make the switch. People tend to stick to the status quo because a passive decision to maintain is easier than an active decision to alter.

The status quo bias is also related to regret: The more active the decision, that is, the more it deviates from the status quo, the more remorse is felt in the event of failure. Even though the pleasure felt from the success of an active decision is greater, we still show a tendency to stick to the status quo and not to change our decisions due to lack of symmetry between pleasure and pain.

A painful example of this is organ donation. In European countries where one must declare in advance if they are willing to be an organ donor, (the countries that appear on the left side of Figure 16,) such as Denmark and Germany, the rates of donors varies between 4%–28%. On the other hand, in European countries where one must declare in advance if they are unwilling to be an organ donor, (appearing on the right side of Figure 16,) such as Sweden and Austria, the rate of donors varies between 86%–100%.

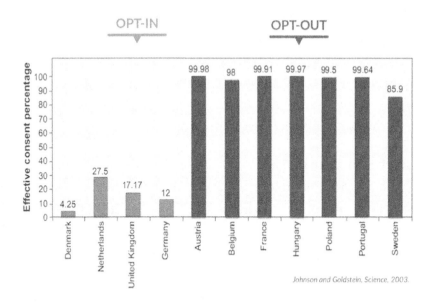

Figure 16—Percentages of organ donors in countries where it is necessary to either declare willingness or unwillingness to be a donor

On the one hand, people don't volunteer to donate organs, but on the other hand, if the law changes and people have to declare explicitly that they don't want to donate, most people will avoid making that declaration, and the result will eventually be that more people will become donors.

Shlomo Benartzi of the University of California and Richard Thaler,who researched decisions related to saving money, reported that there is a huge difference in rates of those who invest in a pension plan that is dependent on a default situation. When the default was "don't invest unless you decide otherwise," the number of those who chose to invest in a pension fund was only 20%. When the default was "invest unless you decide otherwise," the number of people who invested a pension fund rose to 90%.

The tendency to choose the status quo also increases as more choices become available. Amos Tversky and Eldar Shafir asked a group of students which they would prefer:

A. Go to the library and prepare for a difficult exam coming up in two days.
B. Go hear a lecture from their favorite author.

60% chose to go to the library and 40% chose to go to the lecture.

Another group of students was asked which they would prefer:

Go to the library and prepare for a difficult exam coming up in two days.

Go hear a lecture from their favorite author.

Go to a concert of their favorite singer.

80% chose to go to the library. If they chose to go to the lecture, they would regret missing out on the concert, and if they chose to go to the concert, they would regret missing out on the lecture. So let's go study!

Ilan Yaniv and Yaacov Schul of the Hebrew University in Jerusalem conducted several experiments in which a question was asked that had more than one possible correct answers. Some participants were asked to mark which of the answers from a long list were correct, and other participants were asked to mark which were wrong.

For example, the participants were given a description of someone who was a counselor at a Scout camp, volunteered at a hospital, someone who often organized parties and social events, and tended to be independent and make his own decisions. People think of him as a bit "bossy" because he likes to take charge of things. He also works well with other people and is a good team player. It is important for him to choose an occupation that combines independence and a degree of responsibility, and which involves working with other people.

Study participants were asked to choose or to rule out suitable or unsuitable professions from a long list, such as school principal, geneticist, travel agent, diplomat, model, radio reporter, mathematician, and social worker.

From a rational standpoint, we would expect that the grand total of the professions selected as suitable and those selected as unsuitable would be equal to the total number of professions listed. However, studies show that the numbers derived were smaller than all of the professions combined. When people were unsure about whether a profession matched the candidate, they would avoid selecting it, and when people were unsure as to whether the profession didn't match the candidate, they would avoid ruling it out.

Results of the study showed that the "chosen group" at the end of the process was not identical in both decision tasks, and that results were dependent on how the information was sorted. Either way, the resulting group of selections was bigger in the elimination process than in the inclusion process. From here we learn that elimination and inclusion processes are not complementary. This phenomenon also implicates people's willingness to concede during negotiations, as shown in the following study.

Ilan Yaniv, this time with Yifat Maoz and Naama Ivri, received similar results in a study about giving up Israeli settlements for the benefit of the Palestinian Authority. Members of the first group were given a list of 40 settlements located on the other side of the Green Line (West Bank) and were asked to specify which ones they thought should be handed over for the purpose of reaching a peace treaty. Members of the other group received the same list but were asked to mark which settlements they thought should not be given over.

Here, too, the phenomenon repeated itself: The average number of settlements that should be given over and the number of settlements that should be left alone did not amount to the total number of settlements on the list. The list of settlements which the study participants thought should be given over averaged 23 of those that had appeared in the original list when they had to mark which ones should not be relinquished. On the other hand, when participants were asked to mark which should be handed over, only an average of 13 settlements were included in the list. The subjects' recommendations regarding Israel's stance on the matter were also derived from the way the question was posed. The first phrasing led to more moderate positions (willingness to give up more settlements), while the second phrasing led to more stubborn positions (willing to give up fewer settlements).

You can practice this phenomenon with the following question: The list appearing in Table 21 presents names of cities. You are asked to circle cities on the list that you believe **are capital cities**. The actual list of capital cities can be found on page 259. After you do this, turn the page to Table 22 where you will see the same list, and ask someone else to circle all the cities on the list that they believe **are not capital cities**.

Which of the following IS a Capital City?

Abidjan	Dhaka	Mexico City	São Paulo
Amsterdam	Geneva	Monrovia	Shanghai
Auckland	Ho Chi Minh City	Montreal	Sydney
Berlin	Istanbul	Mumbai	Tel Aviv
Buenos Aires	Jerusalem	Nairobi	Toronto
Cairo	Johannesburg	New York	Tripoli
Cape Town	Karachi	Phnom Penh	Washington
Casablanca	Lagos	Pyongyang	Yangon
Colombo	Lima	Quito	Zambia
Dar es Salaam	London	Rio de Janeiro	Zurich

Table 21—List of cities, some of which are capital cities.

In addition to our tendency to remain in the status quo, we also show a tendency to neglect information that evidences that the decision we came to in the past was faulty, and we seek out information that will confirm the decisions we make. This phenomenon is called the **confirmation bias**.

Leeat Yariv from Princeton University goes even further and claims that contrary to the phrase, *"I'll believe it when I see it,"* most people actualize the opposite, in other words, *"I'll see it when I believe it."*

The **confirmation bias** is naturally found in police investigations. Once prime suspects are found, efforts are directed towards convicting them instead of searching for other suspects. Raymond Nickerson states that the **confirmation bias** can be found in every area of life, from witch hunting in the 17th century, to politics, health, and law, up to the latest findings in modern science.

Conclusions:

1. Everybody can do nothing, and people tend to remain in the status quo if it isn't too bad.

2. People dislike change because change is an active deed, something that heightens the intensity of regret in the event of failure (but also pleasure in the event of success).

3. Change means giving up on something that I have for something that I don't have. The pain caused by the loss is usually greater than the pleasure caused by receiving the substitute.

4. The more options there are, the greater the tendency to choose the status quo.

5. Even the act of deliberating change is a decision in and of itself.

6. Regret and pleasure caused as results of a changed decision are greater than those caused as results of an unchanged decision.

7. The expected damage from change seems greater than its expected profit.

8. The bigger the investment in the current situation, the more tendency we will have to remain in it.

9. Instead of searching for reasons that justify previous decisions we made, we should actually be searching for reasons that contradict them.

Which of the following IS NOT a Capital City?

Abidjan	Dhaka	Mexico City	São Paulo
Amsterdam	Geneva	Monrovia	Shanghai
Auckland	Ho Chi Minh City	Montreal	Sydney
Berlin	Istanbul	Mumbai	Tel Aviv
Buenos Aires	Jerusalem	Nairobi	Toronto
Cairo	Johannesburg	New York	Tripoli
Cape Town	Karachi	Phnom Penh	Washington
Casablanca	Lagos	Pyongyang	Yangon
Colombo	Lima	Quito	Zambia
Dar es Salaam	London	Rio de Janeiro	Zurich

Table 22—Another list of the same cities, some of which are capital cities

PART VI

EMOTION
AND INTUITION
IN DECISION MAKING

1

Mental Accounting

A few years ago, I traveled to South America for a series of lectures. I told my wife, "If we're already in South America, let's visit the Galapagos Islands."

"It's very expensive to fly to the Galapagos. Are you earning enough money from the lectures in South America to cover the cost of the trip?"

"No."

"So how will we get there?"

"I will be giving a lecture in a small town near Tel Aviv when we get back to Israel. We'll use the money I receive from there."

My wife opened a mental account in her head called *South America*. The sources for this account are the payments I will receive from the lectures and the uses are the trips, hotels, food, and so on. If the uses are higher than the sources, there's no way to finance the additional trip.

The tendency we have to open a separate account for each event or trip, transaction or stock, and to close it when it reaches a balance is called **mental accounting**. This also describes the tendency to make decisions about certain subjects by neglecting other topics or accounts.

For example, the decision of whether to travel to the Galapagos Islands depends on the proceeds from that same trip and neglects the decision maker's other assets and income.

Mental accounting results from the separation between different sources of money. Upon entering a casino, some people will take money from their wallet, say $200, and put it in their pocket. This is their budget for gambling. Profits made from gambling (if there are any, and usually there aren't) also go into the pocket and not into the wallet. They will comprise separate accounts—a gambling budget. Money from different sources has different objectives. When we lose money that we earned from hard work in the casino, we see this as a loss, but when we lose money in the casino that we won from the casino or from a lotto, or money that we found in the street, we don't view it as a loss.

The wedding is over. The bride changed her dress three times during the ceremony (outfits which cost a total of $9,000). The groom in the white suit, who looks like a Chicago bar singer, sweated all night and smiled elatedly. A flutter of white-winged butterflies flying in from the northwest landed on the bare right shoulder of the bride at the precise second in which the groom uttered, "I do." The guests gorged on the food (which was chosen with great scrutiny by the bride and the groom's mother after many tastings), devouring pheasant meat marinated in pomegranate sauce and artichoke hearts. The DJ (who received $3,000) called out, "Now let's welcome the bride and groom to the dance floor with a round of applause." In short, it looked as though everyone was happy, even though a slight expression of concern appeared on the faces of the groom's mom and the bride's father. They knew that the real test was yet to come.

The young couple returned to the apartment that the bride's parents bought for them (after signing a prenuptial agreement, of course), and the tension reached its peak. The couple stripped off their wedding attire, showered, and the real test began.

The man opened the envelopes and removed the checks, and the woman wrote down the names and sums. The act of marital relations had to wait for the act of money and calculations.

The results were bleak: The expenditures of the wedding reached $51,000 while the value of the gifts reached only $35,000 (if we omit the artsy candlesticks and the original oil painting that one of the guests painted herself), meaning that there was a painful deficit of $16,000. Their joint life journey started off on the wrong foot.

The wife called her parents and told them in bitter tears about the horrible deficit. I could go on and continue describing all the expenditures and revenue, but what does it really matter if the wedding ended in a profit or a loss? Is the wedding a financial deal? Is it a startup investment?

A wedding is an event that costs money and, just like a meal at a restaurant, we pay more for good food. If we order wine, we pay for it as well. Why must we connect the wedding gifts with the cost of the wedding? The "revenue" from the wedding isn't meant to finance the "expenses" of the wedding. We mistakenly open a mental account in our heads called "wedding," which we proceed to charge and credit. When we leave a good meal at a good restaurant, we are likely to say, "That was worth the money." The pleasure from the meal justifies the high price. Why don't we say the same for a wedding?

A man invested money in two stocks: $100,000 in Stock A and another $100,000 in Stock B. Two years later, he needed $50,000. When he checked his account, he noticed that Stock A had dropped 20% and that its current value is only at $80,000, but Stock B rose 10% and its value is at $110,000. As previously mentioned, people tend to sell profiting stocks too quickly and hold on to losing stocks for too long.

Accordingly, the protagonist of our story sold part of his stocks from Company B.

A year later, the man needed money again, this time $40,000. Unfortunately for him, it turned out that Stock A continued to plummet, its value now rested at $65,000, while Stock B rose again by 10% and its value reached $66,000. The man decided to sell Stock B again even though it belonged to a profiting company and he continued holding on to Stock A even though it belonged to a losing company.

And now we will open up a mental account and play out a quiet dialogue between the man and Stock A. "What do you think, that I will sell you at a loss? You wait and see which of us (the man or the stock) will win."

The Stock, as if privy to the teasing, continued going down, and reached a value of only $30,000.

"I won't sell you," said the man to the stock, "at least not until you return to the value at which I bought you."

But all of this accounting is out of place. There is no benefit in calculating the profits of this or any other stock, other than when deciding whether or not to continue investing in it. The goal of buying stocks is to maximize the future profit of the entire portfolio, and not to calculate each share independently.

Kahneman and Tversky asked people the following question, "Imagine that you are about to purchase a jacket for $125 and a calculator for $15. The calculator salesman informs you that the calculator you wish to buy is on sale for $10 at the other branch of the store, located a 20-minutes' drive away. Would you make a trip to the other store?" 68% responded positively.

The second group was asked the following question, "Imagine that you are about to purchase a calculator for $125 and a jacket for $15. The calculator salesman informs you that the calculator you wish to buy is on sale for $120 at the other branch of the store, located a 20-minutes' drive away. Would you make a trip to the other store?" This time only 29% said that they would travel to the other branch.

What is the difference between the two questions? In both cases, you would travel 20 minutes in order to save $5. The difference is that in the first question, the savings were perceived as a one-third reduction of the price of the calculator, while in the second question the relative savings are tiny and stand at only 4%.

As mentioned in previous chapters, the way in which we estimate results is relative and not absolute. Savings are measured in percentages and not in dollars. This, of course, is an error from an economic standpoint—transactions and deeds need to be analyzed and measured according to their absolute financial contribution and not according to their relative contribution.

A group of people were asked the following question, "Imagine that you have decided to see a play and pay the admission price of $10 per ticket. As you enter the theater, you discover that you have lost the ticket. The seat was not marked, and the ticket cannot be recovered. Would you pay $10 for another ticket?" 46% of those asked answered positively.

They asked a second group: "Imagine that you have decided to see a play where admission is $10 per ticket. As you enter the theater, you discover that you have lost a $10 bill. Would you still pay $10 for a ticket for the play?" 88% of the people asked responded positively.

In the first case, we charge the "culture budget" $10. In the second case, we charge the "miscellaneous budget." If we planned on seeing eight plays a year, the loss of the ticket would mean that we only had seven plays left to see. But the loss of the money is not connected at all to the plays.

Thaler distinguishes between **acquisition utility** and **transaction**

utility. Acquisition utility is the rational benefit gained from purchasing something. It is a pleasure caused as a result of the comparison between the product's value and its price. If I am being offered to buy a wireless mouse for $30, I weigh whether the pleasure of having a wireless mouse is worth the payment of $30. If the answer is positive, I buy the product, and if not, I don't.

Unlike acquisition utility, transaction utility is the emotional pleasure that is caused as a result of the comparison between the sum that was paid and some point of reference.

There are people who after buying something abroad will check a local store to see the local price of the product and to learn how much they saved. They will feel immense pleasure if they find out that the price they paid abroad is cheaper than the local price of the product.

Thaler tells the story of a woman who wanted to purchase a cover for her bed. When she arrived at the store, she discovered that the cover she wanted to buy was on sale. There were three sizes: medium, large, and giant. Their prices before the sale were $50, $70, and $80, respectively, but were now all being sold for $30.

The woman's bed was medium-sized, but she purchased the giant cover. She created an equation in her head comparing the old and new prices and felt that the higher the past price of the cover, the more she will gain from the transaction. And she of course couldn't pass up the opportunity to save $50.

Eldar Shafir and Richard Thaler describe in one of their many fascinating articles the following story:

> One of us bought a house recently that came with an industrial, uninsulated stove which violated residential building codes. A protracted search for buyers produced only one promising lead—the owners of a nearby cafe who were

looking to do more cooking. What price should we request for a stove, a couple of years old, originally worth well above $1,000 but worthless to us and with no other buyers on the horizon?

Some friendly bargaining talks (over very good coffee and pastries) soon led to a resolution. They would give us something dear to us but cheap to them: gift coupons to their café.

The ensuing months saw frequent visits to the cafe, with pocketfuls of decorated coupons, each worth $5, and bearing no expiration date. The coffee, the cookies, and the breakfasts felt free. In fact, our many (and growing list of) friends were regularly being offered treats with the usual norms of reciprocity seemingly suspended. Those who did not know about the coupons thought we were wonderfully generous; those who knew, thought it was only fair—in fact, had we made them pay good money while in possession of those "free" coupons, they would have found us petty and cheap.

What was it about those coupons that made them feel so different from the cash we all knew they were worth? Would we have felt equally magnanimous had we lost the coupons rather than used them as intended? Would we have been so generous to our friends had the cafe owners paid us cash for the stove? And when we offered a friend a coupon, would it matter whether that coupon had been purchased at full price or gotten through these other means?

Money doesn't have a scent. Money is money, there's no difference between money that was received from different sources. But in reality, we make clear distinctions between money that was hard-earned and

Maurice Allais

money we found in the street. Coupons we received in lieu of something that we would have gotten rid of anyway doesn't feel like cash to us. Real money that comes out of our pockets is perceived differently than pseudo-money that didn't enter pockets.

About a year ago, I was asked to give a lecture to a group of Mental Health First Aid (MHFA) members in the northern part of Israel. I happily agreed to do it and for free (giving up more than a thousand dollars) out of respect for the wonderful work that they do, but I asked them to cover my travel expenses of $50. Why did I request that they pay for my travel expenses? Could I not have covered the cost myself? Couldn't I see it as a donation to the MHFA?

The answer to the question is connected to the zero illusion which we spoke about in Part V. This is exactly what differentiates between a generous person and a sucker . . . The $1000 that I gave up for the price of the lecture made me feel like a very generous person. This is money that does not enter my pocket. But the $50 that I would have had to take out of my pocket would have made me feel like a sucker.

Here is a story that was told to two groups with a slight difference each time: The price of shoes. The version of the story told to the second group appears in square brackets.

> Imagine that you bought a pair of shoes for $55 about a year ago [for $250 about a year ago. You normally do not spend this much on a pair of shoes, but] You liked the shoes a lot when you bought them and thought you would wear them

often. Alas, you wore them a few times but you found that they hurt your feet. The shoes are still in fashion, but they have now been sitting at the back of your closet unworn for 11 months. You are now putting together some things to donate to the Salvation Army. How likely are you to donate these shoes?

On a scale between 1 (not likely at all) to 7 (very likely), the average of the group who was told the story with the cheaper price was 4.88, and the average of the group who was told the story with the expensive price was only 3.08.

It's much harder for us to donate a pair of shoes that we don't wear and that cost us a fortune then to donate a cheap pair of shoes. The feeling of loss would be greater in the case of the expensive shoes, but in actuality, we're not wearing either pair.

We open mental accounts not only when it comes to money. Calories are another area in which we have the tendency to conduct unnecessary calculations. There are people that break all the diets when they go abroad. "I'm on vacation now!" Just like foreign currency, there are also "foreign calories" which aren't considered in the total count. It's a different account, we tell ourselves. I actually lost weight in the local currency. The weight I gained was in the foreign currency ...

And this is how we act—as if accounts are separate; as if not all the money goes to one pocket, and not all the food reaches one stomach. This is because of the controlling emotional desire to arm oneself against the rigidity of binding logic. When we go on a trip, we're enjoying ourselves and we don't want to think about diets or savings accounts, so we open a new account; one that has no connection to the primary one in the long run. Unfortunately, when we get back home, all of the accounts merge. The bank is the same bank and the stomach is the same stomach. Until the next trip.

Conclusions:

1. Just like after a good meal or a wedding, it's better to be present and enjoy ourselves than to count money.

2. A budget is a decision to take out money. There is no benefit in having a budget in most cases. If there is an expense that seems worthwhile, a budget for it will be found retroactively.

3. If a cup of coffee at the airport costs $8 and we are dying to drink coffee, it doesn't matter how much the cup of coffee costs outside the airport.

4. The goal is to buy what we need inexpensively, and not to buy what we don't need at the maximum sale price.

5. Consumption of a product that was bought a long time ago can sometimes be seen as something free to use or even as something that saves us money.

6. Buying a particular product in advance, such as buying wine a few years before a festive occasion, is seen as an investment rather than an expense.

7. If the product is not consumed as intended, such as a bottle of wine that broke, the bill that has been dormant for a while suddenly comes to life and the expenses involved are now seen as the cost of the product we will need to buy in its place.

8. Ongoing use of a sustainable product such as a private car or a washing machine is not perceived as an expense but as something that is free despite the amortization and the fact that it saves the use of alternative products such as a taxi or a public laundromat.

2

Has Anyone Ever Bought Themselves a Box of Chocolate?

A good friend from work is about to leave for another job. His close friends collected $100 to buy him a going-away present and they decided upon wine since we know our friend appreciates good wine. What would you recommend to buy for the friend:

1. 5 bottles of a type of wine that our friend drinks regularly for $20 a bottle?

2. 2 bottles of exquisite and expensive wine that our friend particularly likes for $50 a bottle?

I asked this question to more than 10,000 people. The vast majority (97%) chose the second option. Most people think it's better to give two expensive bottles of wine rather than five cheap ones.

I made the question more difficult and asked, "And if we give our friend a gift certificate for $100 to buy wine, which would he buy for himself?" Most people said that he would buy the five bottles of cheap wine.

And then I asked, "If we give him the two bottles of expensive wine with a voucher to exchange them for the five cheaper ones, would he

226 | YOSSI YASSOUR

make the switch?" Most people said no.

I continued nagging them, "If we give him the five bottles of cheap wine with a voucher to exchange them for the two cheaper bottles, would he switch them?" Most people answered no.

The majority of people are actually saying that a present should be something special, not something that the recipient regularly consumes, and thus the gift should be the two bottles of expensive wine. A gift is indeed a very special product: It is something that we would be very happy to receive but would usually never buy for ourselves.

A few years ago, the Goodyear Tire and Rubber Company was thinking up ways to incentivize their agents. Management divided the agents into two identical groups. One group was incentivized with money and the other group with gifts of the same monetary value, such as a trip to Hawaii, a year-long membership for NBA basketball games, and so on.

As it turns out, the agents who received the presents raised their tire sales 46% more than those who received the money. One of the reasons for this result is that a present is something that is more tangible than money. It's easier to imagine a Hawaiian vacation than a few extra hundred dollars in the bank.

Richard Thaler asked the following question in one of his studies:

> Imagine you are admiring a $125 cashmere sweater at the department store. You decline to buy it, feeling that it is too extravagant. Later that month, you receive the same sweater as a birthday present from your spouse.
>
> Would you feel happy, indifferent, or angry?

Most of those asked said that they would be very happy to receive the sweater that they wouldn't have purchased themselves. Spending $125 on themselves seems exaggerated but getting a gift for the same sum of money—even though it was bought with their money—actually seems like a good thing. If they would have bought the sweater themselves, they would have perhaps felt regret for overspending, but since their spouse bought the sweater for them, they couldn't feel regret and their attention is focused on the pleasure of having received the sweater and not the pain of the expense.

The classic present is of course a box of chocolates. Has anybody ever seen someone walk into a candy store, pick out a box of chocolates, open it up, and start eating? It seems as though boxes of chocolates weren't intended for consumption but as gifts alone. Ephraim Kishon wrote a short funny story about a man who received a box of chocolates as a gift. When he opened it, he found worms inside. He called the company to complain and they replied, "You opened the box of chocolates? Since when do people open them? It's a present, not food!"

Have you ever seen someone visiting a sick person and bring money for the person to buy the specific kind of chocolates that they like? That would be considered rude. I choose a box of chocolates that I particularly like, visit the sick person, give it to them and say, "So, open it already!"

In the Ruppin Academic Center where I teach, it was customary to receive holiday gifts for Rosh Hashanah (the Jewish New Year) from the institute. They gave us a bottle of red wine, a jar of honey, and a bag of walnuts. Members of the Worker's Committee complained, "Why did they buy red wine? Maybe the workers want white wine. Why honey? Maybe they want jam. Why walnuts? Maybe the workers want almonds." Management decided that they didn't have any patience for the workers' complaints and instead of a holiday gift, they gave the employees gift certificates of the same value as the products they had bought in the past, so that the employees would be troubled with what to purchase and not the company.

Since then, every year, I give my wife the gift certificate. As the family gathers around the beautifully set table on Rosh Hashanah Eve, I ask my wife, "What did you buy with the gift certificate?" And she answers, "The lettuce and the potatoes."

The holiday gift is no more. It is now just a bit of extra cash tacked onto my salary. The additional money gets swallowed up in my bank account and no one ever sees it again.

The rationality of holiday gift-giving has also deteriorated with weddings. No one brings presents anymore. If you ask the bride, "What should I bring?" she will tell you, "Money is best."

Supposedly, gifting money actually is the best option. The young couple will do what they wish with the money. But there is an intellectual and dispassionate point of view here. Most young couples collapse under the pressure of paying back mortgages or student loans. Any money we give them will get lost in these cycles and disappear.

A few years ago, I was invited to the wedding of the son of a very good friend of mine. I know the groom very well and love him very much. The man and his fiancé were avid lovers of the theater. I decided not to give them money for the wedding, but a year-round couples' membership at the National Theatre.

Every now and then when we would meet, they would tell me, "You know, we are stressed beyond belief over our mortgage and loans and we work extra hours nonstop, but once a month we get dressed up, spray on some perfume and aftershave, and go to a play. It's really a treat. We thank you so much that you didn't give us money for the wedding because if you had, we wouldn't be treating ourselves to the theater."

I was of course very happy to hear these words and I was no less pleased when they told me that at the end of the season, that they decided to renew their membership. "If we don't buy a membership, we won't go. The membership forces us to find the time and money to enjoy ourselves."

The young couple's decision brings us to the second subject of this chapter: **self-control**. Richard Thaler, who coined the term **mental accounting**, said, "… the individual can be modeled as an organization with a *planner* and a series of *doers* …" The planner is stable, balanced, composed, and consistent. The doer is selfish and short-sighted. The planner sets rules made to prevent the doer from acting contrary to the planner's long-term preferences. The planner thinks about life as a whole while the doer only thinks about the present. Self-control is like a gift to ourselves but in the opposite direction: Just like we know that we would enjoy a certain gift but we don't buy it for ourselves, we also know that if we are unable to control ourselves, there is a fear that we will be wasteful and break all the rules and all the diets. Therefore, our inner planner (the brain) punishes our inner doer (the body) by denying it the ability to run wild.

It's as if the planner is telling its employer to reduce his salary by a fixed amount and put it in a savings account so that the doer will not be able to waste the money. The planner also distances himself from the box of chocolates or cake so that the doer can maintain the diet which the planner unanimously decided upon, or sends the doer to rehab for smoking or eating. In other words, the planner creates situations that limit the doer's free will.

Here is one way to overcome the gap between the planner's wish and the doer's desire: At the end of the semester, when I give my students their grades, I usually give a 60 (passing grade) to those who received a grade between 50 and 59. I'm aware that the test is only a sample, and I don't want the person who almost passed to be obligated to take the test again if they would be satisfied with earning the minimum grade needed to pass the course.

A student turn to me one day and said:

"I would like for you to please return my original grade of 55 and not change it to 60."

"How come?" I asked in wonder.

"Because I want to take the test again."

"You can still retake the test even if you receive a 60," I told him.

"But if I get a 60, I won't take the test again."

"So don't take the test again."

"But I want to."

"So then take the test again."

"If I have 60, I won't retake it."

The confused student was not satisfied with his grade of 60 and wanted to improve it, but he knew himself well and was aware that if he doesn't force himself to retake the test, he would eventually just give up on it.

For people who acknowledge their weaknesses and fear that they will not meet the task their brains have imposed on them, it is advised to make a public statement of their decision. For example, someone who decides to quit smoking and knows that it will be very difficult, should make it a point to let his friends know about his decision.

A few months ago, I decided, like many times in the past, to stop nibbling on the pretzels that are always left out for free at the college where I work. I knew that I wouldn't follow through unless I made a public declaration, so I hung up a piece of paper on the door to my office which read:

IWNEPARA

Anybody who enters my office always inquires about the meaning of the sign on my door and I tell them it stands for: I Will Not Eat Pretzels At Ruppin Anymore. Indeed, ever since I put that sign on my door, I never touched a pretzel. Wafers are a different story…

In conclusion, our natural tendency is to waste our money without thinking about the long run, to enjoy smoking cigarettes or drinking alcohol without thinking about lung cancer or liver disease. But our logic knows that it is not wise for us. If we don't save money now, we won't have anything to live off of in the future. This is why personal pension plans exist, but even the government makes us invest in our futures through Social Security.

A little nudge

In 2008, a dramatic shift occurred in academic and governmental approaches regarding the issue we are tackling—how decisions can be improved by using tools that change defaults and the status quo. This turning point stemmed from the publication of a book called *Nudge*, written by Richard Thaler, the Nobel laureate in economics in 2017 who has already been mentioned several times throughout this book, and the legal scholar Cass Sunstein. The cover of the book shows an elephant nudging her baby calf along with her trunk. The elephant does not kick her baby forward, but gives it a push—a light one. That's the idea. What is a 'nudge'? A light push, something small in the environment that affects our behaviors and decisions.

The book shows how through a light push, it is possible to get people to behave in a way that is better for them, for the society which they live in, and for the environment. How is it possible to influence people's decisions without using threats, temptations, fines, or discounts—as is customary in our classic economy—but using softer and nonbinding means instead?

Fake flies in the men's room

The most famous example of a nudge is the story about the fly. When men urinate in a public urinal, they generally tend to stand too far from the vertical toilet (due to overconfidence). They hold their phone in their right hand and with their left, they give directions to the person on the other end of the line of how to get there. What's happening below is total chaos. How did they counter this phenomenon at the Schiphol Airport in Amsterdam? They decided to etch an image of a black housefly into the bowls of the airport urinals.

Thaler claims that for evolutionary reasons, when men see a target, they apparently aim right for it. Indeed, after etching the image of a fly into the toilets, spillage was reduced by 80%. In Copenhagen, they marked the path from benches to a nearby garbage bin in a public garden using shoe footprints, thus reducing the amount of litter tossed in the garden by 46%.

In student dormitories in Switzerland, a water meter was installed in the showers to show them how much water they were using, and the amount of water used per shower was reduced from 48 to 40 liters—a 17% reduction.

A light nudge can also come in the form of how food is arranged in the cafeteria. For example, if there are more salads and healthy food served at the beginning of the buffet, people will most likely eat less of the high-fat burgers and calorie-dripping French fries. The assumption is that people want to eat healthy food, but their attraction to delicious food outweighs their need for healthy food.

Crosswalks are also a form of nudging. After all, the driver doesn't want to run over the pedestrian and the pedestrian doesn't want to be run over. The crosswalk guides the drivers, nudging them to pay more attention to the road when they see the street markings. However, there is a problem with this nudging that can cause pedestrians to feel safer and consequently put them more at risk. For example, pedestrians may be less inclined to look both ways before crossing at crosswalks.

In the town where I live, images of children were placed beside crosswalks. The assumption is that drivers will slow down when they see the cut-outs of these children. I fear that drivers living in the area who pass the crosswalk several times and understand that it is a cardboard cut-out and not a real child, will stop driving carefully and eventually run over a real child.

A little nudge to change the status quo

The light push usually works in changing the default. The most researched topic in this area is long-term savings in the United States. Many countries obligate citizens to pay Social Security and thus help people save money for when they reach an old age. In some countries there is no obligation to pay Social Security, and many people who didn't manage to save enough money during their employment period reach an old age without a cent. As a result, some become homeless or move to caravans or distressed neighborhoods.

While the United States government wants people to invest in savings plans and encourages them to save, the liberal view of life doesn't make it possible for people to be forced to save, as has been done in other countries. In the current situation, employers must deduct sums of money from employee salaries to put in a savings plan, but only at the request of the employee.

Thaler and his colleagues suggest that the default should be that each employee has an open savings plan, and that it can be canceled only if they choose to do so. The default should be that the savings plan exists and the employee would have to make an active decision to cancel it, which is already much more difficult. Thaler along with Shlomo Benartzi even went so far as to propose the "Save More Tomorrow" program. This program was designed for people who find it difficult to commit to savings now, to commit to saving in the future, promising that when their salaries increase, they will also increase their savings. Such a plan is easier to digest than having to commit to saving a large sum of money when the salary is relatively low and the living situation is still difficult.

Reversal of decisions from an active to a passive decision

I would now like to suggest a method for making decisions when the results are paramount and the decision itself is hard. I will present this method through a story of something that happened to me a few years ago.

At the Ruppin Academic Center, where I teach, we offer a BA Program for Executives. This is a program designed for people who are relatively older, who work in management positions and have families, and who were unable to study when they were young. I really enjoy teaching in this program since the students are more serious and mature, but even they do not abstain from the incessant and aggressive use of their mobile devices.

One day, a graduate of the program called me and said, "Hello Yossi, I have a difficult decision to make and I would like to discuss it with you."

Requests such as these are not strange to me, because I have always encouraged my students to approach me anytime they want a somewhat objective and professional outlook. The number of requests I have received, including from people who are not my students, has gone up considerably after taking part in a television series called *The Decision*.

The student who called came to me and described her story. "I am 43 years old, happily married, and I have three children: a 19-year-old son who is a soldier, a daughter in 11th grade, and another son who is 13. A week ago, I found out that I was pregnant—which we hadn't planned—and I am deliberating between keeping the baby and getting an abortion. On the one hand, I am a religious woman who is against abortions. On the other hand, I have only just gotten to a point in my life where I can relax from raising children; I have a new and wonderful job, I recently joined a few classes at the community center, and I am thoroughly happy in my current state. What should I do?"

I replied that I was unable to tell her which is the right decision, but that perhaps I could guide her through the decision-making process. I suggested that she switch the decision from an active one to a passive one. I told her, "Imagine that you woke up one morning and realized that you had a miscarriage. You didn't decide or do anything—it happened on its own, by nature, by God. What would be your initial feeling the moment you realize you had a miscarriage? Would you feel relief or sadness? Would you thank God or be angry?"

My intention behind posing this question was to separate the results of the decision from the decision itself. The goal of a decision is the results. The results alone, and not the decision-making process itself, should be a consideration as to whether to go through with something or to avoid it.

If the abortion was indeed initiated, the resulting feeling would be different than if the abortion occurred naturally. That is because in the latter case, feelings of guilt and regret would not arise, but disappointment would. In any event, the suggestion to change the decision from active to passive could, in this case, make it easier for the student to reach a decision.

The dilemmas we tackled while I was participating in this television program were various and far from simple: Should an unwed woman, who carries the gene for breast and ovarian cancer, undergo preventative surgery to remove her ovaries? Should someone who was adopted in infancy open their adoption records? Should a young mother who is in a very difficult financial situation become a surrogate as a source of income? Should parents of children with autism spectrum disorder send them to a special education program or try to integrate them into a regular education framework? Should a young mother who has developed a very successful business give it up in order to become a "perfect" mother? Should an unwed woman over the age of forty give birth to a child alone or give up having children?

I, of course, have no expertise in any of the abovementioned fields, and my role was to help the people with these dilemmas reach a decision in the most organized and objective way possible, through the presentation of different decision-making methods for different circumstances.

From one big passive decision to a sequence of small active decisions
Imagine that just like we have to take our cars for an inspection each year, every married couple would have to renew their weddings vows every year, all over again, signing a declaration that states, "I wish to remain married to him or her for another year." I think that the divorce rates in the U.S., which today stand at around 50%, would probably go up to 80%. The decision to remain married is, as was mentioned, a passive one. If our situation isn't that bad, we will stay. If we were forced to make an active decision every year and go to the courthouse to reaffirm our wedding vows, it could be that this action would awaken sleeping doubts within us, and the deliberation of whether to stay or leave would be harder.

As I write these lines, I am watching the FIFA World Cup. Due to the immense tension and suspense, I eat enormous quantities of cashews to my - and my bloating stomach's - delight. During halftime, I toss the empty bag into the trash and go searching for more.

What have I discovered about myself? That if there is an open bag in the pantry, I immediately devour it. If there is a bag that my wife closed with a clothespin, I devour that one, too. Unfortunately, my wife started attending my public lectures about active and passive decisions, and since then, she has been closing open snack bags by stapling them shut. When this happens, I take out an unopened bag from the pantry, hold it up to my face, recall that I decided to go on a diet 17 years ago, stroke my stomach apologetically, and return the bag to its place.

In a study about dieting and about the correlation between package size and food consumption, Brian Wansink and his colleagues suggested to students—some of whom were thin and some overweight—to watch a comedy on television. At the same time, the researchers placed bags of crackers on the table as a refreshment. In the first group, each participant received one big bag containing 400 calories, and in the second group, each participant received four bags each containing 100 calories. Figure 18 shows the calorie consumption of the thin and overweight participants from each of the two groups.

<Caption> Figure 18—Calorie consumption of thin and overweight participants with one big bag and with four small bags

From Figure 18, we can see that for the thin participants (the right column in each pair), the bag size did not affect their cracker consumption—they ate around 250 calories in both cases. However, there was a big difference in calorie consumption with the overweight participants. When they had four small bags, they ate around 170 calories, and when they had one big bag containing 400 calories, they ate, on average, almost the entire amount—around 390 calories—meaning, consumption was 2.3 times higher compared to when they ate from the small bags.

Eating from an open bag is a passive decision. Opening a closed bag is an active decision. The action behind making the decision is not only measured by the amount of physical energy invested in it, but also—and most importantly—by the degree of mental energy involved.

As mentioned, an active decision is a decision of change, while a passive decision is one of maintaining the status quo. One explanation for resisting change is to avoid making active decisions, avoidance which stems from hating loss, since, as mentioned, the bitterness of failure is double the sweetness of success.

More matters on active and passive decisions; the deviating trolley and the fat man

What you are about to read is one of the most well-known ethical dilemmas in the field of decision making. The two parts to this dilemma are known as the *trolley problem* and *the fat man dilemma.* First, the following dilemma is presented:

> You are standing next to train tracks and notice that the train is moving fast and is about to run over five people working on the tracks. You have the option of pulling a lever that would divert the train down a different track, where it will only run over one worker. Would you pull the lever?

Most people say yes. In the second part, the following dilemma is presented:

> You are standing on a bridge overlooking the track and see that the train is moving fast and is about to run over five people working on the track. Beside you on the bridge is a very fat man. If you push the fat man onto the tracks, the train will run him over and come to a stop, and you will have saved five workers from dying on the tracks. Would you push the fat man to his death?

Most people say no. It should be noted that more men than women "pushed" the fat man onto the tracks. Another disconcerting finding is that people who watched a comedy sketch on television before being presented with the dilemma pushed the fat man over the bridge more than those who did not watch the sketch. An additional finding shows how people were more likely to push a fat man off the bridge than a fat woman.

When it comes to the final result, the two scenarios are identical. The result is 5:1 in both cases. The difference between the two dilemmas is how much action is required to follow through with the act. In the first case, the person pulling the lever is more removed from the event and a rational calculation is more appropriate. In the second case, the decision and the execution are much more active.

This dilemma was also tested in a setting suited to physicians. The following dilemma was presented to a group of doctors:

> In a hospital where you work, you have five patients who require organ transplants—a heart, two kidneys, a pair of lungs, and a liver. Unfortunately, there are no donors and the five patients are about to die. One day, a tourist arrives at the hospital who was slightly injured in a traffic accident. A quick test shows that this tourist is a match for all five patients.

The doctors were asked: Would you kill the tourist and save your five patients? All of the doctors of course answered no. Again, mathematically, the result is 5:1, and that one guy is just a tourist…

On the other hand, if we were to ask a doctor: A tourist died in a traffic accident, and with his organs, you would be able to save five of your patients. Are you happy? I would expect that the doctor would be pleased. However, turning the decision from active to passive won't help in cases where an ethical dilemma arises which the decision maker cannot come to terms with.

An additional point related to the fat man dilemma involves the use of a foreign language. Boaz Keysar and his colleagues found through a series of experiments that the use of a foreign language leads people to put more thought into the problem, and as a result, make more rational and utilitarian decisions, and less decisions that are based on emotion.

They found that when the fat man dilemma was presented in the group's native language, 20% answered that they would push the man to his death, saving the lives of five people. But when the problem was posed in a foreign language which the participants spoke well but wasn't their mother tongue, the rate of those who would push the man over the bridge rose to 33%.

Similar results were found in a related study conducted by Janet Geipel and her colleagues. In Figure 19, we can see that more people (50%–80%) changed the trolley's course and less people (10%–40%) pushed the fat man over the bridge, and in both cases, when the question was asked in a foreign language, the rate of people who operated actively rose. This is especially apparent with the fat man problem, where around 40% pushed him when the question was asked in a foreign language, and only 10% pushed him when it was asked in their native language.

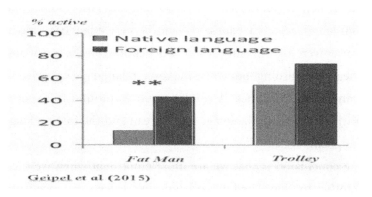

Figure 19—The effect of native and foreign languages on the trolley and fat man problems

Boaz Keysar and his colleagues also examined the effect of foreign language on the Asian disease problem which was presented earlier. A quick reminder: People were asked which vaccine they would prefer to use against an expected epidemic. The decision was between an option with a certain outcome and one with an uncertain outcome, and the results were presented once in a positive way—showing the amount of people who would survive—and once in a negative way—showing the amount of people who would die. Here, too, the language in which the question was posed critically influenced the decision. This can be seen in Figure 20.

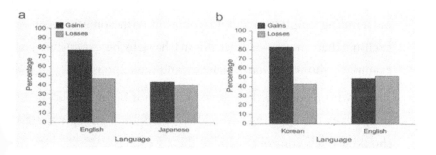

Figure 20—The effect of native and foreign languages on the Asian disease problem

In Experiment A (on the left), the native language was English and the foreign language was Japanese. When the native language was used, responses were significantly different depending on the use of positive and negative wording, but when the foreign language was used, there was almost no difference. A similar result was found in Experiment B, in which the native language was Korean and the foreign language was English.

The conclusion is that we are more emotional when we think in our mother tongue. The foreign language creates a distance from the automatic processes that influence our decisions, enhances our analytical thinking, and minimizes our emotional responses. Therefore, thinking in a foreign language reduces the emotional biases by which we act, including risk avoidance. We tend to take more risks when a foreign language is involved, because fear, which is also an emotion, is reduced.

Conclusions:

1. It's best to give people gifts that will excite them, something they want but don't have to receive, something that doesn't make it to the top of their priorities list, ergo they won't buy it for themselves.

2. Incentivizing methods via monetary bonuses were better suited to coal miners in the 19th century. Managers who want to reward outstanding employees should come up with something more exciting than money—and it doesn't have to be expensive. For example, a dinner with the manager and their spouses.

3. Those who recognize their weaknesses (not being able to wean themselves off smoking, overeating, gambling, shopping, etc.) should use self-control to combat these weaknesses.

4. Apart from decisions regarding health, investing in a pension fund

is perhaps the most important decision for our future. Therefore, we should create an organized and binding plan—such as putting aside a set amount from our present and future income to go towards a fund—which will save us from the human trait of spending today and ignoring tomorrow.

3

Preferences Need No Inferences

Robert Zajonc, a Poland-born Jew, was a psychology professor at Stanford University in California. He became famous in part for his findings that first-born children have higher IQs than their younger siblings. In 1980, he was asked to write an article about the function of emotion in decision-making. The article was commissioned following Zajonc's award for his outstanding scientific contribution in the field of psychology.

The article, which is titled *Feeling and Thinking: Preferences Need No Inferences* was the first to state that our decision-making processes are initially driven by emotion and then by intellect. Initial reactions to stimuli are generally emotional. They appear automatically and subsequently direct the act of processing information and judgment. According to Zajonc, we don't just see a house—we see a beautiful house or an ugly house. Emotion appears automatically without us inviting it and immediately affects how we feel regarding what we see. Zajonc calls this behavior **affect heuristic**: We fool ourselves into believing that during the decision-making process, we act sensibly and weigh the pros and cons. In reality, we buy the car that caught our eye, choose the partner that attracted us, go for the job or home that gave us a good feeling, and only afterwards do we justify our decisions with rational explanations.

Robert Zajonc`

In a different study, Zajonc and colleagues showed people a brief flash of an image of a smiling face, an angry face, or a random geometric shape lasting a fraction of a second. Afterwards, the participants were also shown a drawing of a Chinese ideograph. The participants in the study were asked to say which Chinese ideograph they liked and which they didn't. From the findings, we discover that the Chinese ideographs that were presented after the image of a smiling face were much more favored by the participants than the drawings that were presented after an angry face.

The good feeling that the participants felt in the study caused by the smiling face made them appreciate the drawings more. Our preferences, and even our tastes, alter according to our emotions at the time of evaluation. In a different study, it was reported that a certain type of beer was tastier when the participants felt positive emotion towards it as a result of a positive commercial they saw on TV for that beer.

Antonio Damasio is a neuroscience professor at the University of Southern California hospital. In his book, *Descartes' Error*, he described the behaviors of people whose brain was injured in the region responsible for emotion. The conclusion from his many studies is that while biological drives and emotions may give rise to irrationality, they are indispensable especially in personal and social domains. As he notes, "uncontrolled or misdirected emotions can be a major source of irrational behavior," and knowing the pervasive role of feelings may give us a chance of enhancing their positive effects and reducing their potential harm.

> "… feelings are the sensors for the match … between our nature and circumstance … along with the emotions they come from … they serve us as internal guides … Criteria [for ranking alternatives] are provided by somatic markers, which express … the cumulative preferences we have both received and acquired … somatic markers … forces attention to a possible negative outcome of an action … and thus allow us to choose from among fewer alternatives.

In conclusion, it's not enough to know what should be done, but we must also feel what should be done.

Paul Maslow (not Abraham Maslow from the Hierarchy of Needs) published a book in 1957 titled *Intellect versus Intuition*. Two extreme typecasts are presented in this book—the completely intuitive person and the completely rational person. Here are a few examples of the differences between the two. Which typecast do you relate to more?

> Intuitive people (IP) know at a glance something is right or wrong, good or bad in an absolute overall sense. They grasp "… a situation as a whole without attending to concrete details…" and come to an immediate decision on the basis of {their} current mood. They do not understand why they think in a certain way, only that they do. Intuitive knowledge admits neither question nor doubt.
>
> Rational people (RP), trying to logically understand a totality in all of its parts, engage in an endless struggle to master

details and compare pros and cons. They are reluctant to commit themselves until they laboriously and critically observe, isolate, compare, measure, define and only then, hesitatingly, concede knowing. Striving for a life of pure reason, RP lack spontaneity, liveliness and other qualities that make a refreshing human being.

IP act on inclination and yield to the hand of fate. They do very little planning, sampling life as it comes, savoring each experience here and now, and being aware of the full range of whatever emotion or mood that strikes them.

RP, seeking to control their destiny, have a horror of excessive feelings and act because it is their duty, as part of a plan.

IP rarely argue their beliefs. RP do just that.

RP ask WHY? IP say WHY NOT?

Whereas IP, fearing the non-traditional and the foreign, tend to remain uninvolved when something new appears on the horizon, RP are filled with dynamic curiosity.

IP move from past to present, RP from present to future. IP search for the secret of a happy life in something old and human, RP in something new and modern.

Intellectuality, wonderful in so many ways, is still not enough to encompass the whole of living. Investigation by virtue of "head" alone has been overwhelmingly successful in terms of knowledge about life. But at the same time there is no denying that the gradual shrinkage of the spirit is causing a marked decline in the capacity to enter into truly intimate human relationships. Exclusive cultivation of the intellect dries up the natural sources of feeling, leaving us increasingly insensitive to the elemental pleasures. Something genuinely human is inevitably lost when the artificial displaces the natural. What really counts in living is undermined by an approach that sacrifices biological attachments, historical associations, and intuitive promptings to a lust for scientific discovery.

When intuition and intellect integrate, they cancel out the worst features of each and enhance the constructive energies of the other, to provide us with a balanced presentation of reality.

The following example is very familiar. We know that the top horizontal line is equal in length to the bottom horizontal line. But even though logic "knows" that the horizontal lines are equal in length, we "feel" as though the bottom line is shorter.

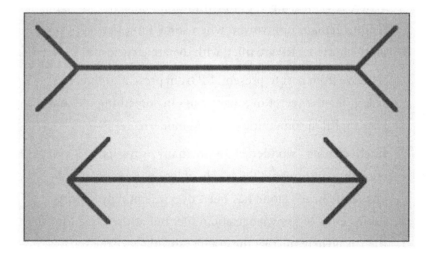

Figure 17—The Müller-Lyer optical illusion

Logic and emotion are constantly at war. Let's discuss the words of the philosopher and researcher of Buddhism and LSD, Alan Watts:

> It is as if we were divided into two parts. On the one hand there is the conscious "I" ... On the other hand there is "me" ... a part of nature ... "I" fancies itself as a reasonable fellow, and is forever criticizing "me" ... for having passions which get "I" into trouble ... and for having appetites which can never be satisfied ... "I" ... will try to make sense of the world ... by attempting to fix it... "I" and "me," the head and the body ... at odds with each other ... [a] war between consciousness and nature, between the desire for permanence and the fact of flux.

> The brain [is] desiring things which the body does not want, and the body [is] desiring things which the brain does not allow; the brain [is] giving directions which the body will not follow, and the body [is] giving impulses which the brain cannot {understand}.

> ... we have been taught to neglect, despise, and violate our bodies, and to put all faith in our brains ... Indeed, the special disease of civilized man might be described as a block or schism between his brain ... and the rest of his body ... We have allowed brain thinking to develop and dominate our lives ... out of all proportion to "instinctual wisdom ..."

There are important advantages to involving emotion in decision-making, but sometimes it negatively affects our choices. I've been wondering for many years if the decision of choosing a partner based on the emotion that is called *love* is better than the matchmaking process in which the primary considerations are rational.

Does emotion sometimes overshadow rationality? Don't we do

things in an emotional frenzy only to later, when our emotions subside and logic finally makes its way into the picture at an annoying snail's pace, regret what we did?

The most important question that man must ask himself in my opinion is: How does one combine conquering emotion with binding logic? Someone who acts solely according to emotion is likely to get carried to places they wouldn't be happy to find themselves in, and someone who acts solely according to logic and seeks explanations for every decision and action is likely to find themselves in a life that lacks challenges.

Jean Buridan, a 14th century French philosopher and priest, is famous for his fable about a rational donkey:

> A rational and starving ass is standing between two identical piles of hay. Unable to choose between the two, the ass dies of hunger.

If someone searches for a logical reason for every decision and action, they are likely to spend their days and nights deliberating and debating and explaining things to themselves and others. Isn't it better to spice up life with a little emotion and not to go through the trouble of understanding and justifying everything?

In a workshop I lead called "The Dynamics of Risk-Taking," which I do with my students at the Dead Sea, there is an exercise of walking on coals. The exercise looks quite scary but it is entirely safe because the walking on coal happens very quickly in two or three steps.

The rational students always ask, "What's it good for?" or say, "Tell me why should I walk on coals from a logical standpoint."

In the end, those who walked on the coals feel satisfaction and excitement, call their loved ones, and tell them about the experience.

Those who didn't do the exercise continue to feel the satisfaction of their rational consistency.

The subject of self-control was mentioned in the previous chapter. Self-control is essentially logic controlling emotion, the brain controlling the body, the preference of long-term over short-term. Daniel Goleman writes about this in his famous book *Emotional Intelligence*:

> In the dance of feeling and thought the emotional faculty guides our moment-to-moment decisions, working hand-in-hand with the rational mind, enabling—or disabling—thought itself. Likewise, the thinking brain plays an executive role in our emotions—except in those moments when emotions surge out of control and the emotional brain runs rampant. [...] The old paradigm held an ideal of reason freed of the pull of emotion. The new paradigm urges us to harmonize head and heart. To do that well in our lives means we must first understand more exactly what it means to use emotion intelligently.

When I was a little boy, my mom would always tell me, "Think before you act" or "Count to 10 before you answer." Why didn't she tell me to feel before I answer? The 50s and 60s were years of rationality. Education was intellect-based, medicine was conventional, and in courts of law, the assumption was that people were rational. This has all shifted in the past few decades. Emotion and intuition have been given a more respectful pedestal. Medicine has become more holistic and more so than in the past, we see that the brain and the body complement each other like yin and yang. A new law was enacted, for example, which states that in the event that a man kills another man after being provoked, it would be considered manslaughter and not murder. Emotion received legal recognition that it didn't have before. In addition to the accepted and widespread idea of IQ which measures mental abilities, EQ has also entered the picture as a measurement of emotional abilities.

Cooper and Sawaf, in their book *Executive EQ: Emotional Intelligence in Leadership and Organizations*, define emotional intelligence as the ability to feel, understand, and apply the intensity of emotions as a source of human energy, information, and influence, and emphasize that it is not a marketing trick and does not deal with the psychology of control, exploitation, or manipulation, but rather with learning, recognition, and evaluation of our emotions and those of others, and the need to respond to them appropriately and to effectively apply the information and power that is expressed in emotion, important decisions, and in daily life.

I will conclude with a model that in my eyes seems to be very updated, demonstrating how we make decisions. This is the dual model of Kahneman and Frederick. According to this model, two systems are at work in our brains: intuitive and rational.

The decision-making process carried out in the intuitive system is automated, effortless, associative, fast and paralleled, dim and skilled. When Bambi hears a noise in the woods, he activates his intuitive system and runs for his life. If he activated his rational system, and took out a pen and paper and began listing all the possible sources of the noise, their chances of harming him, and the potential damage that each source of noise could cause, he would be swallowed up in the gastrointestinal tract of the noise's source before he completes his analytical evaluation.

In contrast to the intuitive process, the rational decision-making process is controlled, strained, deductive, slow and orderly, aware, and follows rules. I visited South Africa a few years ago. I rented a car and proceeded to ride across Cape Town feeling happy and in a kind mood. I soon came to realize the mental differences involved in driving on the left side of the road. Driving took a lot of attention and I was putting a lot of effort into driving on a side of the road I'm not used to driving on. The highlight was when I got to a roundabout. I didn't know if I had to pass the other car on the right or the left. I had to stop and follow a different car.

In my home country, my driving is automatic. I hardly have to think or put any effort into it. Sometimes I don't recall driving for a few miles because my mind was bothered with other matters. The system that operates while driving regularly differs from the one that operates while driving under unfamiliar conditions, as on the left side of the road.

According to the theory of the dual model for decision making, in the first stage of each decision, the intuitive system offers a quick solution. In phase two, the rational system examines the quality of the intuitive system's suggestions, and then accepts, corrects, or rejects them.

A person is considered spontaneous or intuitive if they act in the end according to what they felt at the beginning. If the changes that the rational system imposes on the intuitive system are many, and the final decision differs significantly from the quick intuitive decision, the person is said to be calculated and rational.

Take a look at the three forms in Figure 18.

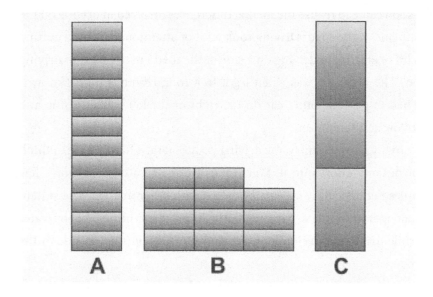

Figure 18— Observation of the heights and areas of the three forms

The observation that Rectangle A is equal in height to Rectangle C is made automatically and very speedily. The process of identifying this fact is intuitive, muffled, and effortless. In contrast, the observation that the area of Shape B is equal to the area of Rectangle C is contrived and slow. This is a rational and conscious process that requires effort.

The following three questions will illustrate the topic. You are asked to answer them as quickly as possible, then to go to page 259 to see the correct answers.

Question 1

A tennis racket and a tennis ball cost $11 together.
The racket cost $10 more than the ball.
What is the price of the ball?

Question 2

Lily pads grow in the lake.
Their area doubles in size daily.
Within 48 days, the plants will cover the entire lake.
Within how many days will the plants cover half the
surface of the lake?

Question 3

A man cuts a baguette into four equal pieces over a
span of four seconds.
How many seconds will it take to cut the baguette
into 16 equal pieces?

Was your answer to the first question $1?
Was your answer to the second question 24 days?
Was your answer to the third question 16 seconds?

Go to page 259 and look at the correct answers.

Sometimes the intuitive solution is correct and sometimes the rational system quickly corrects the wrong intuitive solution. Errors in judgment and decision making occur only when the intuitive system provides an incorrect solution and the rational system doesn't notice the error and doesn't correct it.

In conclusion, it can be said that either way, emotion and intuition should not be replaced when it comes to making complex decisions. Sigmund Freud said, "When making a decision of minor importance, I have always found it advantageous to consider all the pros and cons. In vital matters, however, such as the choice of a mate or a profession, the decision should come from the unconscious, from somewhere within ourselves. In the important decisions of personal life, we should be governed, I think, by the deep inner needs of our nature."

In my opinion, modern man's mission is to find the golden path between the conquering emotion and the binding logic; to decide (rationally) when to use emotion for decision making and when to use intellect, when to act intuitively and when to hesitate, consult, plan, and only then act.

Conclusions:

1. The first reactions to stimuli are usually emotional responses. They appear automatically, and later direct the act of processing information and judgment.

2. We fool ourselves into thinking that we choose a logical path and examine the pros and cons when in reality, we decide according to emotion and then justify our choices with logical explanations.

3. When we were kids, they told us to think before we answer. Today, we might want to tell our children that they should both think and feel before they decide.

4. Rationality, as wonderful as it is, is not enough to encompass all areas of life.

5. Reducing emotion in decision making leads to a decrease in the ability to have intimate relationships.

6. Exclusive cultivation of intellect may dry up our natural sources of emotion and reduce our sensitivity to basic pleasures.

7. The really important things in life may get lost when the artificial

replaces the natural and when intuitive sensations and biological emotions are sacrificed on the altar of lust for scientific discovery.

8. When intuition and intellect join together, they eliminate each other's disadvantages and reinforce each other's advantages and give the person a more balanced picture of himself and of reality.

9. Emotion sabotages decisions when it inspires fear and restraint precisely when courage and perseverance are necessary.

10. In order to be good managers, better partners, and better people in general, we should get to know and appreciate our feelings and those of others and respond to them appropriately. That may be why women, who combine emotion with decisions more than men, also make better managers.

For Pages 84-85

1	The Capital of USA is?	**Washington**
2	Population of Indonesia is?	**240M**
3	The "Magic Flute" was composed by	**Mozart**
4	The distance between London and Paris (km)	**350**
5	Tegucigalpa is the Capital of	**Honduras**
6	Which Book of the Old Testament has more chapters?	**Isaiah**
7	Number of commercial flights per day in the USA	**30000**
8	The Capital of Morocco is?	**Rabat**
9	The Currency of Nepal is?	**Rupee**
10	The "Beatles" were from	**England**
11	Number of babies born per day around the world	**370000**
12	Potatoes are native of	**Peru**
13	Out of 2300 snakes number of poisonous is?	**400**
14	Population of Iceland is?	**350000**
15	In the USA more people die of	**Diabetes**
16	The chance of contracting AIDS in 1 <u>unprotected</u> heterosexual episode from a partner who has Aids is	**0.2%**
17	Majority of Cocoa production is in	**Africa**
18	Which country produces more rice	**India**
19	Which country has more policemen/1000 people	**Italy**
20	Number of Muslims in the world	**2.1B**

For page 77

Minimum and Maximum Values of 1000 people

Phrase	Minimum	Personal	Maximum
Almost Certain	60%		99%
Good Chance	51%		95%
No Doubt	80%		100%
Probably	30%		90%
No Chance	0%		35%
Frequently	20%		90%
Expected	40%		100%
Low Probability	1%		40%

For page 52

Countries beginning with the letters C and I.

C	I
Cambodia	Iceland
Cameroon	India
Canada	Indonesia
Cape Verde	Iran
Central African R.	Iraq
Chad	Ireland
Chile	Israel
China	Italy
Colombia	
Comoros	
Congo R.	
Costa Rica	
Côte d'Ivoire	
Croatia	
Cuba	
Cyprus	
Czech R.	
17	8

For page 212

Capital Cities

Berlin
Buenos Aires
Cairo
Dhaka
Jerusalem
Lagos
Lima
London
Mexico City
Monrovia
Nairobi
Phnom Penh
Pyongyang
Quito
Tripoli
Washington

For page 255

$$X+Y = 11$$
$$X-Y = 10$$

$$X = 10.5$$
$$Y = 0.5$$

$$48-1 = 47$$

Cutting a baguette into four pieces takes four seconds and 3 cuts. Cutting the baguette into 16 pieces requires 15 cuts, which is 5 times it took to cut it into 4 slices. 5X4 = 20 Seconds.

REFERENCES

Alcock, J. (1975). Territorial Behavior by Males of Philanthus Multimaculatus with a Review of Territoriality in Male Sphecids. *Animal Behaviour* 23(4), pp. 889-890.

Ariely, Dan. (2008). Predictably Irrational : the Hidden Forces That Shape Our Decisions. HarperCollins

Ariely, D., Huber, J., & Wertenbroch, K. (2005). When Do Losses Loom Larger than Gains? *Journal of Marketing Research* 42(2), pp. 134-138.

Ariely, D., & Kreisler, J. (2017). Dollars and Sense, How We Misthink Money and How to Spend Smarter. Harper Collins Publishers.

Arkes, H. R., & Blumer, C. (1985). The Psychology of Sunk Cost. Organizational Behavior and Human Decision Processes 35, pp. 124-140.

Arkes, H. R., Kung, Y., & Hutzel, L. (2002). Regret, Valuation, and Inaction Inertia. Organizational Behavior and Human Decision Processes 87, pp. 371-385.

Armstrong, J., Friesdorf, R., & Conway, P. (2018). Clarifying Gender Differences in Moral Dilemma Judgments: The Complementary Roles of Harm Aversion and Action Aversion. *Social Psychological and Personality Science, doi:1948550618755873.*

Bar-Eli, M., Azar, O., Ritov, I., Keidar-Levin, Y., & Schein, G. (2007). Action Bias among Elite Soccer Goalkeepers: The Case of Penalty Kicks. *Journal of Economic Psychology* 28(5), pp. 606-621.

Baron, J., & Ritov, I. (1994). Reference Points and Omission Bias. *Organizational Behavior and Human Decision Processes,* 59(3), pp. 475-498.

Baron, J., & Ritov, I. (2004). Omission Bias, Individual Differences, and Normality. *Organizational Behavior and Human Decision Processes* 94, pp. 74-85.

Baumeister, R. F., Bratslavsky, E., Finkenauer, C., & Vohs, K. D. (2001). Bad is Stronger than Good. *Review of General Psychology* 5, pp. 323-370.

Baumeister, R. F., & Tierny, J. (2011). *Willpower: Rediscovering the Greatest Human Strength.* Penguin Press.

Beike, D. R., Markman, K. D., & Karadogan, F. (2009). What We Regret Most are Lost Opportunities: A Theory of Regret Intensity. *Personality and Social Psychology Bulletin 35,* pp. 385-397.

Bell, D. E. (1982). Regret in Decision Making under Uncertainty. *Operations Research* 30, pp. 961-981.

Benartzi, S., & Thaler, R. H. (1995). Myopic Loss Aversion and the Equity Premium Puzzle. *The Quarterly Journal of Economics* 110(1), pp. 73-92.

Benartzi, S., & Thaler, R. (2007). Heuristics and Biases in Retirement Savings Behavior. *Journal of Economic Perspectives* 21(3), pp. 81-104.

Bergman, P., Lasky-Fink, J., & Rogers, T. (Working Paper). Simplification and Defaults Affect Adoption and Impact of Technology, But Decision Makers Do Not Realize This.

Brenner, L., Rottenstreich, Y., Sood. S., & Bilgin, B. (2007) On the Psychology of Loss Aversion: Possession, Valence, and Reversals of the Endowment Effect. *Journal of Consumer Research* 34, pp. 369-376.

Carmon, Z., & Ariely, D. (2000). Focusing on the Forgone: Why Value Can Appear So Different to Buyers & Sellers. *Journal of Consumer Research* 27(3), pp. 360-370.

Chan, M. Y., Cohen, H., & Spiegel B.M.R. (2009). Fewer Polyps Detected by Colonoscopy as the Day Progresses at a Veteran's Administration Teaching Hospital. *Clinical Gastroenterology and Hepatology* 7(11), pp. 1217-1223.

Costa, A., Foucart, A., Hayakawa, S., Aparici, M., Apestguia, J, Heafner, J, & Keysar, B. (2014). Your Morals Depend on your Language. *PLoS One. e94842.*

Dai, H., Milkman, K.L., Hofmann, D.A., & Staats, B.R. (2015). The Impact of Time at Work and Time off from Work on Rule Compliance: The Case of Hand Hygiene in Healthcare. *Journal of Applied Psychology* 100(3), pp. 846-862.

Danziger, S., Levav, J., & Avnaim-Pesso, L. (2011). Extraneous Factors in Judicial Decisions, *Proceedings of the National Academy of Sciences* 108(17), pp. 6889-6892.

Dobelli, R. (2013). *The Art of Thinking Clearly*. Farrar, Straus & Giroux.

Donovan, R. J., & Jalleh, G. (2000). Positive versus Negative Framing of a Hypothetical Infant Immunization: The Influence of Involvement. *Health Education and Behavior* 27(1), pp. 82-95.

Edmonds, D. (2013). *Would You Kill the Fat Man? The Trolley Problem and What Your Answer Tells Us about Right and Wrong*. Princeton University Press.

Erev, I., Ert, E., & Yechiam, E. (2008). Loss Aversion, Diminishing Sensitivity, and the Effect of Experience on Repeated Decisions. *Journal of Behavioral Decision Making* 21(5), pp. 575-597.

Ert, E., & Erev, I. (2008). The Rejection of Attractive Gambles, Loss Aversion, and the Lemon Avoidance Heuristic. *Journal of Economic Psychology* 29, pp. 715-723.

Ert, E., & Erev, I. (2013). On the Descriptive Value of Loss Aversion in Decisions under Risk: Six Clarifications. *Judgment and Decision Making* 8(3), pp. 214-235.

Esteves-Sorenson, C., & Perretti, F. (2012). Micro-Costs: Inertia in Television Viewing. *Economic Journal* 122, pp. 867-902.

Gailliot, M. T., & Baumeister, R. F. (2011). The Physiology of Willpower: Linking Blood Glucose to Self-Control. *Personality and Social Psychology Review* 11, pp. 303-327.

Genesove, D., & Mayer, C. (2001). Loss Aversion and Seller Behavior: Evidence from the Housing Market. *The Quarterly Journal of Economics* 116(4,1), pp. 1233-1260.

Geipel, J., Hadjichristidis, C., & Surian, L. (2015). How Foreign Language Shapes Moral Judgment. *Journal of Experimental Social Psychology* 59, pp. 8-17.

Gilovich, T., & Medvec, V. H. (1995). The Experience of Regret: What, When, and Why. *Psychological Review* 102, pp. 379-395.

Gottman, J. (1995). *Why Marriages Succeed or Fail: And How You Can Make Yours Last.* Simon & Schuster.

Green, J. D. (2016). Solving the Trolley Problem, in *A Companion to Experimental Philosophy*, Sytsma, J. & Buckwalter, W. (Ed.), John Wiley & Sons, pp. 175-178.

Green, J. D., Morelli, S. A., Lowenberg, K., Nystrom, L. E., & Cohen, J. D. (2008). Cognitive Load Selectively Interferes with Utilitarian Moral Judgment. *Cognition* 107(3), pp. 1144-1154.

Halpern, S. D., Ubel, P. A., & Asch, D. A. (2007). Harnessing the Power of Default Options to Improve Health Care. *New England Journal of Medicine* 357, pp. 1340-1344.

Hammond, J. S. (1967). Better Decisions with Preference Theory. *Harvard Business Review* 45(6), pp. 123-141.

Hardie, B. G., Johnson, E. J., & Fader, P. S. (1993). Modeling Loss Aversion and Reference Dependence Effects on Brand Choice. *Marketing science* 12(4), pp. 378-394.

Hartman, R., Doane, M., Woo, C. K. (1991). Consumer Rationality and the Status Quo. *Quarterly Journal of Economics* 106, pp. 141-162.

Hayakawa, S., & Keysar, B. (2018). Using a Foreign Language Reduces Mental Imagery. *Cognition* 173, pp. 8-15.

Hill, C., Memon, A., & McGeorge, P. (2008). The Role of Confirmation Bias in Suspect Interviews: A Systematic Evaluation. *Legal and Criminological Psychology* 13, pp. 357-371.

Hsee, C. K. (1998). Less is better: When Low-value Options are Valued More Highly than Vigh-value Options. *Journal of Behavioral Decision Making* 11, pp. 107-121.

Hochman, G., & Yechiam, E. (2011). Loss Aversion in the Eye and in the Heart: The Autonomic Nervous System's Responses to Losses. *Journal of Behavioral Decision Making* 24(2), pp. 140-156.

Imas, A., Sadoff, S., & Samek, A. (2016). Do People Anticipate Loss Aversion? *Management Science* 63(5), pp. 1271-1284.

Inzlicht, M., & Marcora, S. M. (2016). The Central Governor Model of Exercise Regulation Teaches Us Precious Little about the Nature of Mental Fatigue and Self-Control Failure. *Frontiers in Psychology* 7, p. 656.

Inzlicht, M., & Schmeichel, B. J. (2012). What is Ego Depletion? Toward a Mechanistic Revision of the Resource Model of Self-Control. *Perspectives on Psychological Science* 7, pp. 450-463.

Inzlicht, M., Schmeichel, B. J., & Macrae, C. N. (2014). Why Self-Control Seems (but may not be) Limited. *Trends in Cognitive Science, 18,* 127-133.

Isoni, A. (2011). The Willingness-to-Accept/Willingness-to-Pay Disparity in Repeated Markets: Loss Aversion or 'Bad-Deal' Aversion? *Theory and Decision, 71(3),* 409-430.

Johnson, E. J., & Goldstein, D. (2003). Do Defaults Save Lives?" *Science* 302, pp. 1338-1339.

Johnson, E. J., & Goldstein, D. (2013). Decisions by Default. *The Behavioral Foundations of Public Policy,* ed. Shafir, E., Princeton University Press, pp. 417-427.

Johnson, E. J., Haubl, G., & Keinan, A. (2007). Aspects of Endowment: A Query Theory of Value Construction. *Journal of Experimental Psychology: Learning, memory, and cognition* 33(3), pp. 461-474.

Johnson, E. J., Shu, S. B., Dellaert, B. G., Fox, C., Goldstein, D. G., Häubl, G., & Schkade, D. (2012). Beyond Nudges: Tools of a Choice Architecture. *Marketing Letters* 23(2), pp. 487-504.

Juraskova, I., O'Brien, M., Mullan, B. Bari, R, Laidsaar-Powell, R., McCaffery, K. (2012). HPV Vaccination and the Effect of Information Framing on Intentions and Behavior: An application of the Theory of Planned Behavior and Moral Norm. *International journal of behavioral medicine* 19 (4), pp. 518-525.

Kahneman, D. (2011). Thinking, Fast and Slow. New York: Farrar, Straus and Giroux.

Kahneman, D., Knetsch, J. L., & Thaler, R. H. (1990). Experimental Tests of the Endowment Effect and the Coase Theorem. *Journal of political Economy* 98(6), pp. 1325-1348.

Kahneman, D., Knetsch, J., & Thaler, R. (1991). Anomalies: The Endowment Effect, Loss Aversion, and Status Quo Bias. *Journal of Economic Perspectives* 5(1), pp. 193-206.

Kahneman, D., & Miller, D. T. (1986). Norm Theory: Comparing Reality to Its Alternatives. *Psychological Review* 93, pp. 136-153.

Kahneman, D., & Tversky, A. (1979). Prospect Theory: An Analysis of Decision under Risk. *Econometrica*, 47, pp. 263-291.

Kahneman, D., & Tversky, A. (1984). Choices, Values, and Frames. *American Psychologist* 39(4), pp. 341-350.

Kassin, S. M., Dror, I. E, & Kukucka, A. (2013). The Forensic Confirmation Bias: Problems, Perspectives, and Proposed Solutions. *Journal of Applied Research in Memory and Cognition* 2, pp. 42-52.

Kassin, S. M., Goldstein, C. C., & Savitsky, K. (2003). Behavioral Confirmation in the Interrogation Room: On the Dangers of Presuming Guilt. *Law and Human Behavior* 27, pp. 187-203.

Keeney, R. L., & Raiffa, H. (1976). *Decisions with Multiple Objectives.* Wiley.

Kermer, D. A., Driver-Linn, E., Wilson, T. D., & Gilbert, D. T. (2006). Loss Aversion is an Affective Forecasting Error. *Psychological Science* 17, pp. 649-653.

Keysar, B., Hayakawa, S., & An, S. G., (2012). The Foreign Language Effect: Thinking in a Foreign Tongue Reduces Decision Biases. *Psychological Science* 23, pp. 661-668.

Klayman, J., & Ha, Y. W. (1997). Confirmation, Disconfirmation, and Information in Hypothesis Testing. *Psychological Bulletin* 94, pp. 211-228.

Knetsch, J. (1989). The Endowment Effect and Evidence of Nonreversible Indifference Curves. *American Economic Review* 79, pp. 1277-1284.

Koehler, J. J. (1993). The Influence of Prior Beliefs on Scientific Judgments of Evidence Quality. *Organizational Behavior and Human Decision Processes* 56, pp. 28-55.

Kressel, L. M., & Chapman, G. B. (2007). The Default Effect in End-of-Life Medical Treatment Preferences. *Medical Decision Making* 27, pp. 299-310.

Kruger, J., Wirtz, D., Van Boven, L., & Altermatt, T. W. (2004). The Effort Heuristic. *Journal of Experimental Social Psychology* 40(1), pp. 91-98.

Larrick, R. P., & Soll, J. B. (2008). The MPG Illusion. *Science* 320(5883), pp. 1593-1594.

Levin, I. P., Schneider, S. L., & Gaeth, G. J. (1998). All Frames are Not Created Equal: A Typology and Critical Analysis of Framing Effects. *Organizational Behavior and Human Decision Processes* 76(2) pp. 149-188.

Levin, I. P., Schreiber, J., Lauriola, M., & Gaeth, G. J., (2002). A Tale of Two Pizzas: Building Up from a Basic Product Versus Scaling Down from a Fully-Loaded Product. *Marketing Letters* 13(4), pp. 335-344.

Linder, J. A., Doctor, J. N., Friedberg, M. W., Reyes Nieva, H., Birks, C., Meeker, D., & Fox, C. R. (2014), Time of Day and the Decision to Prescribe Antibiotics. *Journal of the American Medical Association, Internal Medicine* 174(12), pp. 2029-2031.

Loomes, G., & Sugden, R. (1982). Regret Theory: An Alternative Theory of Rational Choice under Uncertainty. *Economic Journal* 92, pp. 805-824.

Loewenstein, G., Bryce, C., Hagmann, D., & Rajpal, S. (2015) Warning: You are about to Be Nudged. *Behavioral Science and Policy* 1(1), pp. 35-42.

Maoz, I., Yaniv, I., & Ivry, N. (2007). Decision Framing and Support for Concessions in the Israeli-Palestinian Conflict. *Journal of Peace Research* 44, pp. 81-91.

Mazar, N., Shampanier, K., & Ariely, D. (2017). When Retailing and Las Vegas Meet: Probabilistic Free Price Promotions. *Management Science* 63(1), pp. 250-266.

McGraw, A. P., Larsen, J. T., Kahneman, D., & Schkade, D. (2010). Comparing Gains and Losses. *Psychological science* 21(10), pp. 1438-1445.

McKenzie, C. R., Liersch, M. J., & Finkelstein, S. K. (2006). Recommendations Implicit in Policy Defaults. *Psychological Science* 17, pp. 414-420.

McNeil, B. J., Pauker, S. G., Sox H. C., & Tversky, A. (1982). On the Elicitation of Preferences for Alternative Therapies. *New England Journal of Medicine* 306, pp. 1259-1262.

Medvec, V. H., Madey, S. F., & Gilovich, T. (1995). When Less is More: Counterfactual Thinking and Satisfaction among Olympic Medalists. *Journal of Personality and Social Psychology* 69(4), pp. 603-610.

Mukherjee, S., Sahay, A., Pammi, V. C., & Srinivasan, N. (2017). Is Loss-Aversion Magnitude-Dependent? Measuring Prospective Affective Judgments Regarding Gains and Losses. *Judgment and Decision Making* 12(1), pp. 81-89.

Mullainathan, S., & Shafir, E. (2013). *Scarcity: Why Having Too Little Means So Much*. Times Books/Henry Holt and Co.

Nayakankuppam, D., & Mishra, H. (2005). The Endowment Effect: Rose-Tinted and Dark-Tinted Glasses. *Journal of Consumer Research* 32(3), pp. 390-395.

Nickerson, R. S. (1998). Confirmation Bias: A Ubiquitous Phenomenon in Many Guises. *Review of General Psychology* 2(2), pp. 175-220.

Norton, M. I., Mochon, D., & Ariely, D. (2012). The IKEA Effect: When Labor Leads to Love. *Journal of Consumer Psychology* 22, pp. 453-460.

Novemsky, N., & Kahneman, D. (2005). The Boundaries of Loss Aversion. *Journal of Marketing Research,* 42(2), pp. 119-128.

O'Brien, B. (2009). Prime Suspect: An Examination of Factors that Aggravate and Counteract Confirmation Bias in Criminal Investigations. *Psychology, Public Policy and Law* 15, pp. 315-334.

O'Keefe, D. J., & Jensen, J. D. (2007). The Relative Persuasiveness of Gain-Framed Loss-Framed Messages for Encouraging Disease Prevention Behaviors: A Meta-Analytic Review. *Journal of Health Communication* 12(7), pp. 623-644.

Odean, T. (1998). Are Investors Reluctant to Realize Their Losses? *The Journal of finance* 53(5), pp. 1775-1798.

Pink, D. H., (2018). *When: The Scientific Secrets of Perfect Timing,* Riverhead Books.

Prelec, D., & Loewenstein, G. (1998). The Red and the Black: Mental Accounting of Savings and Debt. *Marketing science* 17(1), pp. 4-28.

Raiffa, H. (1968). *Decision Analysis: Introductory Lectures on Choices under Uncertainty.* Addison-Wesley.

Ritov, I. (1996). Probability of Regret: Anticipation of Uncertainty Resolution in Choice. *Organizational Behavior and Human Decision Processes* 66, pp. 228-236.

Ritov, I., & Baron, J. (1990). Reluctance to Vaccinate. *Journal of Behavioral Decision Making* 3, pp. 263-277.

Ritov, I., & Baron, J. (1992). Status-quo and Omission Bias. *Journal of Risk and Uncertainty* 5, pp. 49-61.

Ritov, I., & Baron, J. (1995). Outcome Knowledge, Regret, and Omission Bias. *Organizational Behavior and Human Decision Processes* 64, pp. 119-127.

Ritov I., & Baron, J. (1999). Protected Values and Omission Bias. *Organizational Behavior and Human Decision Processes* 97, pp. 79-94.

Roese, N. J., & Summerville, A. (2005). What We Regret Most...and Why. *Personality and Social Psychology Bulletin 31,* pp. 1273-1285.

Rozin, P., & Royzman, E. B. (2001). Negativity Bias, Negativity Dominance, and Contagion. *Personality and social psychology review* 5(4), pp. 296-320.

Samuelson, W., & Zeckhauser, R. (1988). Status Quo Bias in Decision Making. *Journal of Risk and Uncertainty* 1, pp. 7-59.

Shampanier, K., Mazar, N., & Ariely, D. (2007). How Small is Zero Price? The True Value of Free Products. *Marketing Science* 26, pp. 742-757.

Schwartz, B., Ward, A., Monterosso, J., Lyubomirsky, S., White, K., & Lehman, D. R. (2002). Maximizing Versus Satisficing: Happiness Is a Matter of Choice. *Journal of Personality and Social Psychology* 83(5), pp. 1178-1197.

Schweitzer, M. (1994). Disentangling Status Quo and Omission Effects: An Experimental Analysis. *Organizational Behavior and Human Decision Processes* 58(3), pp. 457-476.

Shani, Y., Danziger, S., & Zeelenberg, M. (2015). Choosing between Options Associated with Past and Future Regret. *Organizational Behavior and Human*

Decision Processes 126, pp. 107-114.

Shani, Y., & Zeelenberg, M. (2007). When and Why Do We Want to Know? How Experienced Regret Promotes Post-Decision Information Search. *Journal of Behavioral Decision Making* 20(3), pp. 207-222.

Simenson, I. (1992). The Influence of Anticipating Regret and Responsibility on Purchase Decisions. *Journal of Consumer Research* 19, pp. 105-118.

Simonson, I., & Drolet, A. (2004). Anchoring Effects on Consumers' Willingness-to-Pay and Willingness-to-Accept. *Journal of Consumer Research* 31(3), pp. 681-690.

Steffel, M., Williams, E. F., & Pogacar, R. (2016). Ethically Deployed Defaults: Transparency and Consumer Protection via Disclosure and Preference Articulation. *Journal of Marketing Research* 53, pp. 865-880.

Suri, G., Sheppes, G., Schwartz, C., & Gross, J. J. (2013). Patient Inertia and the Status Quo Bias: When an Inferior Option Is Preferred. *Psychological Science* 24(9), pp. 1763-1769.

Talluri, B. C., Urai, A. E., Tsetsos, K., Usher, M., & Tobias H. Donner, T. H. (2018). Confirmation Bias through Selective Overweighting of Choice-Consistent Evidence. *Current Biology* 28(19), pp. 3128-3135.

Teger, A. I. (1980). *Too Much Invested to Quit*. Pergamon.

Thaler, R. (1980). Toward a Positive Theory of Consumer Choice. *Journal of Economic Behavior and Organization* 39, pp. 36-90.

Thaler, R. H. (1985). Mental Accounting and Consumer Choice. *Marketing Science* 4, pp. 199-214.

Thaler, R. H. (2000). From Homo Economicus to Homo Sapien. *The Journal of Economic Perspectives,* 14(1), pp. 133-141.

Thaler, R. H. (2015). *Misbehaving: The Making of Behavioral Economics*. W.W. Norton & Company.

Thaler, R. H., & Benartzi, S. (2004). Save More Tomorrow™: Using Behavioral Economics to Increase Employee Saving. *Journal of political Economy* 112(S1), pp. S164-S187.

Thaler, R. H. & Rosen, S. (1976). The Value of Saving a Life: Evidence from the Labor Market, in *Household Production and Consumption*, N. E. Terleckyj (ed.), pp. 265-302.

Thaler, R. H. & Shefrin, H. M. (1981). An Economic Theory of Self-Control. *Journal of Political Economy 89*, pp. 392-406.

Thaler, R. H. & Sunstein, C. R. (2008). *Nudge: Improving Decisions about Health, Wealth, and Happiness*. Yale University Press.

Thomson, J. (1985). The Trolley Problem. *Yale Law Journal* 94(6), pp. 1395-1415.

Tiefenbeck, V., Goette, L., Degen, K., Tasic, V., Fleisch, E., Lalive, E., & Staake, T. (2018). Overcoming Salience Bias: How Real-Time Feedback Fosters Resource Conservation. *Management Science* 64(3), pp. 1458-1476.

Tversky, A., & Kahneman, D. (1981). The Framing of Decisions and the Psychology of Choice. *Science* 211, pp. 453-458.

Tversky, A., & Kahneman, D. (1986). Rational Choice and the Framing of Decisions. *Journal of Business* 59(4), pp. S251-S278.

Tversky, A., & Kahneman, D. (1991). Loss Aversion in Riskless Choice: A Reference Dependent Model. *The Quarterly Journal of Economics* 106(4), pp. 1039-1061.

Tykocinski, O. E., Israel, R., & Pittman, T. S. (2004). Inaction Inertia in the Stock Market. *Journal of Applied Social Psychology* 34, pp. 1166-1175.

Tykocinski, O. E., Pick, D., & Kedmi, D. (2002). Retroactive Pessimism: A Different Kind of Hindsight Bias. *European Journal of Social Psychology* 32, pp. 577-588.

Tykocinski, O. E., & Pittman, T. S. (1998). The Consequences of Doing Nothing: Inaction Inertia as Avoidance of Anticipated Counterfactual Regret. *Journal of Personality and Social Psychology* 75, pp. 607-616.

Tykocinski, O. E., Pittman, T. S., & Tuttle, E. S. (1995). Inaction Inertia: Foregoing Future Benefits as a Result of an Initial Failure to Act. *Journal of Personality and Social Psychology* 68, pp. 793-803.

Tykocinski, O. E., & Steinberg, N. (2005). Coping with Disappointing Outcomes: Retroactive Pessimism and Motivated Inhibition of Counterfactuals. *Journal of Experimental Social Psychology* 41, pp. 551-558.

Vadillo, M. A., Gold, N., & Osman, M. (2016). The Bitter Truth about Sugar and Willpower: The Limited Evidential Value of the Glucose Model of Ego Depletion. *Psychological Science* 27, pp. 1207-1214.

Van Putten, M., Zeelenberg, M., van Dijk, E., & Tykocinski, O. E. (2013). Inaction Inertia. *European Review of Social Psychology* 24, pp. 123-159.

Walasek, L., & Stewart, N. (2015). How to Make Loss Aversion Disappear and Reverse: Tests of the Decision by Sampling Origin of Loss Aversion. *Journal of Experimental Psychology: General* 144(1), pp. 7-11.

Wansink, B., Payne, C. R., & Shimizu, M. (2011). The 100-Calorie Semi-Solution: Sub-Packaging Most Reduces Intake among the Heaviest. Obesity 19(5), pp. 1098-1100.

Wason, P. C. (1968). Reasoning about a Rule. *Quarterly Journal of Experimental Psychology* 20(3), pp. 273-281.

Weaver, R., & Frederick, S. (2012). A Reference Price Theory of the Endowment Effect. *Journal of Marketing Research* 49(5), pp. 696-707.

Winter, E. (2014). *Feeling Smart: Why Our Emotions More Rational than We Think*, Public Affairs Publishing.

Winter, E. (2015). Loss Aversion and Romance: Why Do We Search More for Deal Breakers than for Positive Trait in Partners? *Psychology Today.* (November).

Yaniv, I., & Schul, Y. (1997). Elimination and Inclusion Procedures in Judgment. *Journal of Behavioral Decision Making* 10(3), pp. 211-220.

Yaniv, I., & Schul, Y. (2000). Acceptance and Elimination Procedures in Choice: Non–Complementarity and the Role of Implied Status Quo. *Organizational Behavior and Human Decision Processes* 82(2), pp. 293-313.

Yassour, Y. (2021). *100% Right 50% of the Time: How to Prevent Fallacies in Decision Making.* Amazon Books.

Yechiam, E., Ashby, N. J., & Pachur, T. (2017). Who's Biased? A Meta-Analysis of Buyer-Seller Differences in the Pricing of Lotteries. *Psychological Bulletin* 143(5), pp. 543-563.

Yechiam, E., & Hochman, G. (2013). Losses as Modulators of Attention: Review and Analysis of the Unique Effects of Losses over Gains. *Psychological bulletin* 139(2), pp. 497-518.

Zamir, E. (2012). Loss Aversion and the Law. *Vanderbilt Law Review* 65, pp. 829-894.

Zamir, E., & Ritov, I. (2012). Loss Aversion, Omission Bias, and the Burden of Proof in Civil Litigation. *The Journal of Legal Studies* 41(1), pp. 165-207.

Zamir, E., & Teichman, D. (2018). *Behavioral Law and Economics,* Oxford University Press.

Zeelenberg, M. (1999). Anticipated Regret, Expected Feedback and Behavioral Decision Making. *Journal of Behavioral Decision Making* 12, pp. 93-106.

Zeelenberg, M., Nijstad, B. A., van Putten, M., & van Dijk, E. (2006). Inaction Inertia, Regret, and Valuation: A Closer Look. *Organizational Behavior and Human Decision Processes* 101, pp. 89-104.

Zeelenberg, M., & Pieters, R. (2007). A Theory of Regret Regulation 1.0. *Journal of Consumer Psychology* 17(1), pp. 3-18.

Zlatev, J. J., Daniels, D. P., Kim, H., & Neale, M. A. (2017). Default Neglect in Attempts at Social Influence. *Proceedings of the National Academy of Science* 114 (52), pp. 13643-13648.